Mountain Biking Hut to Hut:
Telluride to Moab

Help Us Keep This Guide Up to Date

Every effort has been made by the author and editors to make this guide as accurate and useful as possible. However, many things can change after a guide is published—trails are rerouted, regulations change, facilities come under new management, etc.

We would love to hear from you concerning your experiences with this guide and how you feel it could be improved and kept up to date. While we may not be able to respond to all comments and suggestions, we'll take them to heart and we'll also make certain to share them with the author. Please send your comments and suggestions to the following address:

The Globe Pequot Press
Reader Response/Editorial Department
P.O. Box 480
Guilford, CT 06437

Or you may e-mail us at:

editorial@GlobePequot.com

Thanks for your input, and happy trails!

A FALCON GUIDE®

Mountain Biking Hut to Hut: Telluride to Moab

Stephen Hlawaty

FALCON®

GUILFORD, CONNECTICUT
HELENA, MONTANA

AN IMPRINT OF THE GLOBE PEQUOT PRESS

*A***FALCON**GUIDE®

Text design by Nancy Freeborn
All interior photos by the author except where noted.

ISSN 1549-3687
ISBN 0-7627-3092-7

Manufactured in the United States of America
First Edition/First Printing

Contents

Mountain Biking Hut to Hut

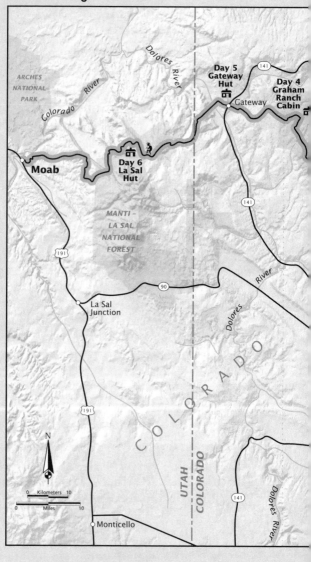

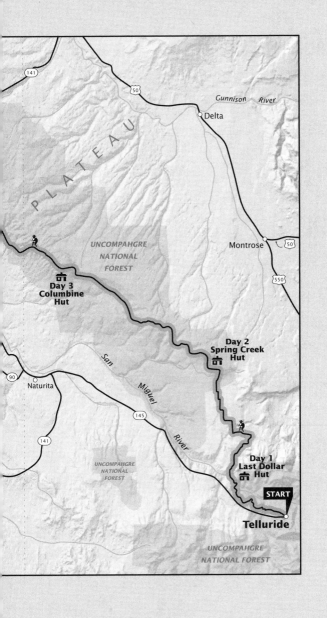

Acknowledgments

Curtis Church, Jeremy Moore, Peter Boniface, mountain biking hut to hut with you guys through the wilds of southern Colorado and Moab, Utah, was a blast. Thanks. A special tip-of-the-hat to Pete for duct-taping the Jim Beam traveler to the frame of his bike. On behalf of all of us, thank you for that.

A heartfelt thank you goes out to my wife Amanda Hlawaty. You stepped up big on this trip and represented with quiet strength. It's good having you on this side of the hill.

Introduction

The San Juan Hut System follows a long-standing tradition of backcountry travel, a tradition whose roots span over 8,000 years and stretch across the world. The thirteenth-century Mongol warlord Genghis Khan knew well that comfort is key to conquest and drew upon that knowledge when he created the largest land empire in history, stretching from the Caspian Sea to the Sea of Japan. Mongolians would shelter themselves in their *gers*—the Mongolian term for "home"— as they traveled across the steppes of central Asia in conquest. These round, self-supporting shelters of wood and felt are still being used today by Mongolians moving their herds from northern Mongolia's Darhad Valley to winter pasture near Lake Hovsgol. This centuries-old, weeklong trek crosses over 10,000-foot, snowcapped mountains and travels over 70 miles.

Asia's European neighbors have also adopted a similar tradition, albeit much more luxurious and elegant, in their haute routes. One classic haute route travels from Cha- monix, France, and the base of Europe's tallest mountain, 15,770-foot Mont Blanc, to Zermatt, Switzerland, and the base of the 14,691-foot Matterhorn. First completed on foot by the Alpine Club in 1861, much of this haute route would later be developed as a ski route by Joseph Ravenal and his party of ski-mountaineers in 1903. However, due to the technical and dangerous nature of crossing the Plateau du Couloir, the ski route was never fully completed, that is, until the mountaineering pioneers Marcel Kurz and Professor

1

Roget made the first successful crossing of the couloir in 1911. Designed primarily as a backcountry ski tour, this haute route includes 90 miles of alpine travel in ten days.

It didn't take long for this backcountry travel tradition to cross the Atlantic and secure a place for itself in North America. Built in 1904, New Hampshire's Carter Notch Hut is perhaps the country's oldest all-season mountaineering hut. It would take twelve more years before Colorado could claim its own hut reserved primarily for backcountry enthusiasts. Fern Lake Lodge, a cabin in Rocky Mountain National Park, has been providing shelter for backcountry travelers since 1916. But the first true hut to be used as a skier's base camp was created in the late 1940s, when Billie Taggert and his skiing buddies restored an old miner's cabin located at the head of Castle Creek near Aspen. This hut would eventually be rebuilt and become part of the Alfred Braun Memorial Hut System—Colorado's oldest ski-oriented hut system.

Today Colorado offers outdoor enthusiasts the largest and most diverse selection of hut systems in the lower forty-eight states. Equipped with all the amenities for comfortable living—fuel, pots and pans, cookstoves and wood-burning stoves, lanterns, bedding, games—backcountry huts deliver a secure and secluded backcountry experience. Most of these huts are privately run on land leased from the national forests. Present-day huts now provide year-round, backcountry refuge for outdoor enthusiasts interested in hiking, skiing, camping, fishing, hunting, and, most recently, mountain biking.

Hut-to-hut mountain biking offers riders a unique opportunity to venture deep into, and stay within, the wilds of Colorado's backcountry. It combines one of childhood's fondest memories—riding your bike—with one of adulthood's strongest passions—enjoying the Colorado outdoors. While there are several hut-to-hut tour operators within Colorado that provide huts accessible by mountain bike, the San Juan Hut System stands as Colorado's original mountain bike hut-to-hut tour operator, one whose route crosses the Colorado state line into Utah.

The San Juan Hut System's seven-day mountain bike tour from Telluride, Colorado, to Moab, Utah, travels over 200 miles. This tour is the granddaddy of all Colorado hut-to-hut mountain bike tours. And with stories of it appearing in *Men's Journal* and *National Geographic Adventure,* it may well be the country's premier hut-to-hut mountain bike tour. With this kind of exposure, this classic mountain bike tour is gaining in popularity. Indeed the San Juan Hut System huts can become 100 percent full throughout the entire riding season, with 125 days in a row booked solid. Such an increase in business has prompted San Juan Hut System owner and operator Joe Ryan to approach the National Forest Service to expand his business by creating a second mountain bike route from Durango, Colorado, to Moab, Utah. This new route will open in the summer of 2004.

This book serves as your guide in planning your Telluride to Moab mountain biking adventure. While staying in a different San Juan Hut System hut each day of the week on your way from Telluride to Moab is principally what makes this tour unique, you could also use this book as a guide to plan your own self-supported tour, since the entire route passes through federal lands. Those wishing to opt out of staying in the San Juan Hut System's huts should identify appropriate campsite locations along the route.

Whichever way you choose to use this guide, there is no mistaking the San Juan Hut System's place among the pioneers in a long-standing hut-to-hut tradition. It seems fitting that an American invention—mountain biking—should have as its classic tour one that connects the two best mountain biking destinations in America: Colorado and Utah. And with that in mind, enjoy the ride.

How to Use This Book

Stuffed with plenty of useful information, *Mountain Biking Hut to Hut: Telluride to Moab* features seven mapped and cued rides as well as everything from advice on what to bring to tips on mountain bike repair and maintenance.

What You'll Find in This Guide

Each day starts with a ride summary. This summary gives you a taste of the adventures that will be featured on this ride. You'll learn about the trail terrain and what surprises the route has to offer.

The ride specs follow the summary. Here you'll find the quick, nitty-gritty details of each day of the ride: where you will start, ride distance, approximate riding time, difficulty rating, type of trail terrain, the nearest town, what other trail users you may encounter, and, for Days 3 and 5, alternate singletrack routes. Our Getting There sections for Days 1 and 7 give you dependable directions from a nearby city right down to where you'll want to park. The Ride section is the meat of the chapter. Detailed and honest, it's the author's carefully researched impression of the trail. Although it's impossible to cover everything, you can rest assured that we won't miss what's important. In our Miles and Directions section we provide mileage cues to identify all turns and trail name changes, as well as points of interest. Between this and our route map, you simply can't get lost.

This book uses elevation profiles to provide an idea of the length and elevation of hills you will encounter along each ride. In each of the profiles, the vertical axes of the graphs show the distance climbed in feet. In contrast, the horizontal axes show the distance traveled in miles. It is important to understand that the vertical (feet) and horizontal (miles) scales can differ between rides. Read each profile carefully, making sure you read both the height and distance shown. This will help you interpret what you see in each profile. Some elevation profiles may show gradual hills to be steep or steep hills to be gradual.

How to Use These Maps

We don't want anyone, by any means, to feel restricted to just the roads and trails that are mapped here. We hope you will have an adventurous spirit and use this guide as a platform to dive into Colorado's backcountry and discover new routes for yourself. One of the simplest ways to begin this is to just turn the map upside down and ride the course in reverse. The change in perspective is fantastic, and the ride should feel quite different. With this in mind, it will be like getting two distinctly different rides on each map.

For your own purposes, you may wish to copy the directions for the course onto a small sheet to help you while riding, or photocopy the map and cue sheet to take with you. These pages can be folded into a bike bag or stuffed into a jersey pocket. Just remember to slow or even stop when you want to read the map.

Map Legend

⑤ Interstate Highway	✝ Airfield	⚓ Golf Course
⑧ U.S. Highway	✈ Airport	杨 Hiking Trail
③ State Road	🚲 Bike Trail	🛒 Mine
㉓ County Road	🚫 No Bikes	☇ Overlook
45 Forest Road	⇌ Boat Launch	🎋 Picnic
Paved Road	)(Bridge	🅿 Parking
Paved Bike Lane	🚏 Bus Stop	✕ Quarry
Maintained Dirt Road	⚠ Campground	(ᴀ) Radio Tower
Unmaintained Jeep Trail	⚑ Campsite	勇 Rock Climbing
Singletrack Trail	⚓ Canoe Access	🏫 School
Highlighted Route	☰ Cattle Guard	🏠 Shelter
Ntl Forest/County Boundaries	✝ Cemetery	⎁ Spring
State Boundaries	✝ Church	⚓ Swimming
Railroad Tracks	⛪ Covered Bridge	器 Train Station
Power Lines	⤳ Direction Arrows	⋔ Wildlife Refuge
Special Trail	⛷ Downhill Skiing	🌿 Vineyard
Rivers or Streams	🗼 Fire Tower	◆◆ Most Difficult
Water and Lakes	✝ Forest HQ	◆ Difficult
Marsh	⟿ 4WD Trail	☐ Moderate
	⥮ Gate	● Easy

Great Escape Telluride to Moab: Hut to Hut

Day 1: Telluride to Last Dollar Hut
Day 2: Last Dollar Hut to Spring Creek Hut
Day 3: Spring Creek Hut to Columbine Hut
Day 4: Columbine Hut to Graham Ranch Cabin
Day 5: Graham Ranch Cabin to Gateway Hut
Day 6: Gateway Hut to La Sal Hut
Day 7: La Sal Hut to Moab

Telluride to Moab: Hut to Hut

Trail contacts: San Juan Hut System, P.O. Box 773, Ridgway, CO 81432; (970) 626–3033; www.sanjuanhuts.com. Kaibab Mountain Bike Tours, 391 South Main Street, Moab, Utah; (435) 259–7423, (800) 451–1133; www.kaibabtours.com.
Schedule: June 1 to October 1.
Fees and permits: Through the San Juan Hut System, it's $475 per person for a seven-day, self-guided hut-to-hut tour from Telluride to Moab.
Maps: *DeLorme Colorado Atlas & Gazetteer:* page 76, A-2 to A-3; page 66, D-1 to B-2; page 65, B-7 to A-4; page 55, D-4; page 54, D-4 to C-1—continued in *DeLorme Utah Atlas & Gazetteer:* page 41, D-6 to D-4; page 31, A-5 to A-3; Uncompahgre National Forest Map and the Manti–La Sal National Forest Map.

The Ride

Riders taking part in the San Juan Hut System's Telluride to Moab bicycle tour are in for an epic adventure. Expect to be treated to the 14,000-foot, snowcapped peaks of the San Juans, the 100-mile Uncompahgre Plateau, the awe-inspiring canyons of the Dolores River Valley, the rugged La Sal Mountains rising high above the red plain deserts of Moab, and the surreal red-rocked canyons and mesas of Moab. Save for the few singletrack trails that spur from the main route, the trip from the one-time tent city of Telluride to the legendary outlaw town of Moab is more a test of stamina than of mountain bike handling skills.

Riders typically travel for seven days, mostly along U.S. Forest Service and Bureau of Land Management roads in the Uncompahgre and Manti–La Sal National Forests, staying in

Packing up for the Great Escape.

a different hut each night. Situated along the route, these huts stand anywhere from 13 to 38 miles apart and include all the comforts of home. The six huts are equipped with eight padded bunks, a propane cookstove, propane lights, a wood-burning stove (except for the Gateway and La Sal huts), and kitchen facilities. Although there is no running water, all huts include a water supply for drinking and cooking. The hut is stocked with dry and canned goods, some fresh fruit and vegetables, spices, sleeping bags, and even beer if you're lucky.

Mike Turrin and Joe Ryan, Telluride locals, started the San Juan Hut System and their Telluride to Moab hut-to-hut trip in 1988. Since then this trip has amassed classic status among fat tire enthusiasts. Riders receive three meals a day, lodging, and miles of jaw-dropping views. And if that doesn't sell you, try adding a 7,000-foot vertical drop from the Last Dollar Hut, atop Last Dollar Pass, and a cold glass of beer at the Moab Brewery into the mix. All this and more can be yours for just $475 per person. That's $67.85 per day.

Although riders are given a minimum-suggested equipment list and route descriptions, this hut tour is designed to be self-guided. Riders are expected to be in good physical shape and have knowledge of backcountry safety, first aid, and bicycle repair. A consideration often overlooked when assessing one's physical ability is the extra weight carried along this trip. Since this route travels through remote mountain territory, expect the unexpected, particularly weather—which can range from sweltering heat to snowstorms. You'll need to equip yourself with a bicycle repair kit, first-aid kit, hydration system or at least three large bottles of water, rain gear, a full layering system (shirt, hat, gloves, socks, separate pair of shoes), and bug repellent. The added weight of these items, coupled with the length and elevations of some of the day's rides, may greatly reduce an individual's stamina. Please know your limits.

From Telluride, the Victorian mining town tucked deep in the corner of a San Juan box canyon, riders ascend Last Dollar Pass along the western edge of the Sneffels Range. From there, it's a savage descent to Buck Canyon (for a more remote route, the San Juan Hut System recently made Price Canyon its preferred dry season route) and Howard Flats before connecting with the Uncompahgre Plateau, a massive mesa whose sides are cut by huge gorges. Riding west atop the entire length of the plateau's spine, riders descend via a knuckle-wrenching road into the Dolores River Valley. From deep in the heart of the valley, a long and arduous climb up

HUT-TO-HUT BIKING

There are hut-to-hut trips available throughout the country. Most, however, are booked six to twelve months in advance. Here is a short list of other hut-to-hut outfitters you might be interested in contacting.

The Yurts of Never Summer Nordic, P.O. Box 1903, Fort Collins, CO, 80502; (970) 482-9411. May 1 to October 1. Situated on the eastern flank of North Park in the Colorado State Forest, the Never Summer Nordic yurts are canvas, tent-like structures. There are as many as five yurts to which you can ride. Although kitchen facilities are provided, you must bring your own food, water, and sleeping bags. Rates range from $45 to $75 per person per night.

10th Mountain Hut System, 1280 Ute Avenue, Suite 21, Aspen, CO, 81611; (970) 925-5775; www.huts.org. Aspen to Vail, Colorado. July 1 to September 30. Surrounding the Holy Cross Wilderness Area, this system includes eleven huts between Aspen and Vail. Most of the huts are $22 per person per night and include sleeping bunks and kitchen facilities. Riders must bring their own food. Guided tours are available.

John Brown Canyon awaits, as riders head toward the Utah border and the La Sal Mountains. From the La Sal Mountains, it's a fast-paced ride down into Moab, where millions of years of wind, water, and erosion have carved some of the country's most startling landscapes.

This kind of mountain bike tour includes some momentous gems you might not otherwise consider. Conversations

Just desserts on top of Last Dollar Pass.

with riding companions range from the day's sorest bum to the unrivaled benefits of being in Colorado and the spectacular lunar-scaped scenery of Utah and its high deserts. The days tend to pass quickly as you ride, eat, sleep, and ride again. In between the rhythm of the days, you may find the time to harmonize with friends during a heated wood-chopping competition. Not seeing your own reflection for a week, enduring unexpected rain delays, and meeting the challenge of making a new and exciting meal at the end of each day are just a few of the interesting times shared by all.

Although most of the riding is nontechnical, there are a lot of singletrack rides you can do. Consult with the San Juan Hut System for more information on these and other available alternatives. With the Telluride-to-Moab mountain bike tour becoming as popular as it is, would-be vacationers should reserve their spaces early, probably three to six months in advance. Reservations are made through the San Juan Hut System at (970) 626–3033.

Ride Information for Telluride

Local Information

Telluride Visitor Center, 666 West Colorado Avenue, Telluride; (970) 728-6265, (800) 525-2717.

Ridgway Area Chamber of Commerce, 150 Racecourse Road, Ridgway, CO, 81432; (970) 626-5181, (800) 220-4959.

Outermost Adventures, Telluride; (970) 626-5491 for shuttles and pick-up service.

Visitors Information on Telluride, www.telluride.com.

Local Events and Attractions

Telluride Bluegrass Festival, in June (contact Telluride Visitor Center, 970-728-6265, 800-525-2717).

Melee in the Mines Mountain Bike Races, in July (contact Telluride Visitor Center, 970-728-6265, 800-525-2717).

Wild Mushrooms Conference, in August (contact Telluride Visitor Center, 970-728-6265, 800-525-2717).

Film Festival, in September (contact Telluride Visitor Center, 970-728-6265, 800-525-2717).

Blues & Brews Festival, in September (contact Telluride Visitor Center, 970-728-6265, 800-525-2717).

Accommodations

Town Park and Campground, 500 East Colorado Avenue, Telluride; (970) 728-2173 ($11 per night camping; showers and toilet facilities available May 15 to October 15).

Restaurants

La Cocina De Luz, 123 East Colorado Avenue, Telluride; (970) 728-9355 (Mexican take-out and catering company).

Rustico Ristorante, 114 East Colorado Avenue, Telluride; (970) 728-4046.

Smuggler's, 101 West San Juan Avenue, Telluride; (970) 728-0919 (Telluride's only brewpub).

Tours

Telluride Outside, 1982 West Highway 145, Telluride; (970) 728-3895, (800) 831-6230; www.tellurideoutside.com.

Back Country Biking, Telluride; (970) 728-0861.

Telluride Sports/Adventure Desk, 150 West Colorado Avenue, Telluride; (970) 728-4477, (800) 828-7547.
Telski/Mountain Adventures, Telluride; (970) 728-6900.

Shipping Bikes
Parragon Ski & Sports, Telluride; (970) 728-4525 (contact Michael Brown, owner).

Ride Information for Moab

Local Information
Moab, Green River Visitors Center, Moab; (800) 635-6622.
Moab Chamber of Commerce, 805 North Main Street, Moab, UT, 84532; (435) 259-7814.
Visitors Information on Moab, www.moabutah.com.

Local Events and Attractions
Canyonlands National Park, (435) 259-7164.
Arches National Park, (435) 259-8161.

Accommodations
Free camping along the Colorado River
Slickrock Campground, 1301½ North U.S. Highway 191; (435) 259-7660, (800) 448-8873.

Restaurants
Moab Brewery, 686 South Main (next to McDonald's), Moab; (435) 259-6333.
Grand Old Ranch House, 1266 North U.S. Highway 191, Moab; (435) 259-5753.
La Hacienda, 574 North Main, Moab; (435) 259-6319.
Eddie McStiff's, 57 South Main, Moab; (435) 259-BEER.
Moab Diner, 189 South Main, Moab; (435) 259-4006 (great milkshakes).

Tours
Dreamride Tours, Moab; (888) MOAB-UTAH; www.dream ride.com.
Never Summer Western Spirit Cycling, Moab; (800) 845-2453.
Nichols Expedition, 497 North Main, Moab; (801) 259-3999; www.NicholsExpeditions.com.
O.A.R.S/North American River Expeditions, 543 North Main, Moab; (800) 342-5938; www.oars.com.
Holiday Expeditions, Inc., 544 East 3900 South, Salt Lake City, Utah; (801) 266-2087, (800) 624-6323; www.bikeraft.com.

Day 1 **Telluride to Last Dollar Hut**

One of the most scenic and most photographed Colorado back roads, Last Dollar Road, leads to the Last Dollar Hut. Last Dollar Hut overlooks the La Sal Mountains and Utah to the west, the Wilson Peaks and the Lizard Head Wilderness Area to the south, and the Silverton West Group of the San Juan Mountains to the east. While the route is not particularly long, it does climb steeply at high elevations, and it delivers challenging switchbacks as you near Last Dollar Pass at 11,000 feet. Once you reach the pass, you're greeted with a 300-vertical-foot hike-a-bike section to the hut itself. View this as your final payment for one of Colorado's most exquisite panoramic views.

Start: From downtown Telluride.
Distance: 13.7 miles.
Approximate riding time: Advanced riders, 2 to 3 hours; intermediate riders, 3 to 4 hours.
Technical difficulty: Technically easy to moderate. Much of the route travels on well-maintained paved and dirt roads. There are a couple of talus-field crossings with which you'll have to contend.
Physical difficulty: Physically moderate to challenging due to the sustained and steep climbs at high elevations. The final approach to the Last Dollar Hut is particularly demanding.
Terrain: Paved bike path, paved road, and dirt road. The terrain encountered includes loose talus-field rock, sand, and dirt.
Nearest town: Telluride, Colorado.
Other trail users: Hikers, backpackers, sightseers, and photographers.

Getting there: From Telluride, Colorado: Drive west on Colorado Avenue to Mahoney Drive. Turn left onto Mahoney Drive, passing

The crew setting out on Last Dollar Road.

Prospect and Smuggler Streets to your left, and bear right into the Coonskin parking lot at the base of the Coonskin Lift (Lift 7). Park your vehicle here and begin riding.

The Ride

At around 10:00 A.M. on June 24, 1889, Butch Cassidy, Tom McCarty, and Matt Warner robbed the San Miguel National Bank in Telluride, forever labeling this Telluride depository as the first bank Butch Cassidy ever robbed. After their successful gunpoint withdrawal, the "Wild Bunch" took to the hills with the loot. Destination? Moab, Utah. They were headed to Brown's Hole, located in a large valley along the foot of Diamond Mountain, near the Green River of Utah. In his autobiography, Tom McCarty spoke of their first hit.

"Our plans were accordingly laid very carefully to go to a certain bank [San Miguel National Bank of Telluride, which handled large mine payrolls] and relieve the cashier of his ready cash." The plan involved following a secret route from Telluride to Moab, with food and supplies located at key hideouts along the way. The threesome had even taken time to train the horses to stand perfectly still while each man vaulted into the saddle.

To aid in their getaway, Cassidy enlisted the services of his younger brother, Dan Parker. Parker served as supply runner. He'd travel ahead of the outlaws and drop stores of food and supplies at prearranged locations along the route—an important consideration if one hoped to cross the rugged San Juan and La Sal Mountains successfully. No one doubted the Wild Bunch's ability to get away, even with a reputed $30,000 weighing them down—they were all accomplished riders—but Butch's little brother didn't fare so well. Parker was arrested while transporting the supplies. He was brought to Wyoming to answer to these and older charges. His subsequent arrest and imprisonment forced Cassidy, McCarty, and Warner to fend for themselves.

As for Butch and his gang, they were never found, nor was the stolen money. The posse employed to track the outlaws was not as enthusiastic about the chase as might be expected. The Wild Bunch were legendary gunmen, and word of their pistol skills, no doubt, preceded them wherever they went. Telluride's Sheriff Beattie, masking his shame for never having captured the gang, resorted to boasting about the one thing he did manage to capture: Butch's horse. For years after the robbery, Sheriff Beattie delighted himself by riding around downtown Telluride on Butch Cassidy's horse, the only one that didn't get away.

Day 1 Telluride to Last Dollar Hut

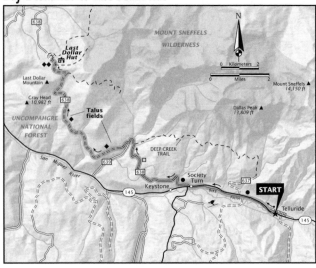

Today, riders can travel a similar route on their getaway from Telluride to Moab. By replacing saddlebags with panniers and horses with mountain bikes, riders can relive what it must have been like for Butch and his gang, riding from one food and supply hideout to the other. You begin your escape by riding up Telluride's Last Dollar Road, across the western corner of the Sneffels Range, to your first night's hideout, Last Dollar Hut. Although the 13.7-mile stretch from Telluride to the Last Dollar Hut is the shortest leg (in terms of miles) of the weeklong getaway, it climbs an impressive 2,500 feet to Last Dollar Pass (11,000 feet).

The Last Dollar Hut, the highest hut along the route and one of the first to be built in the San Juan Hut System, sleeps eight and sits atop a wind-beleaguered ledge, overlooking the sheep-grazing meadows below. The Last Dollar Hut offers one of the most dramatic panoramic vistas in Colorado. From the perch you can take in views of the Silverton West Group of the San Juans, the La Sal Mountains in Utah (Day 6), and the Wilson Peaks (Mount Wilson, 14,246 feet, and Wilson Peak, 14,017 feet). The Wilson Peaks are perhaps the most prominent.

Mount Wilson and Wilson Peak were named after the famed topographer of the Hayden Survey Team. To have even one of Colorado's fifty-four Fourteeners named after you would be an incredible honor, but to have two peaks bear your name is almost unimaginable. A. D. Wilson is so honored. Wilson's list of accomplishments includes doing topographic work with Clarence King's 14th Parallel Survey, being the second to ascend Mount Rainier (within weeks of the first), and helping to organize the Hayden Atlas. The Hayden Survey Team was one of the first teams to accurately survey Colorado in the mid-1800s. Their extensive research and study were included in the Hayden Atlas. It was, however, primarily Wilson's work with the Hayden Survey Team that ensured him his place among the highest peaks of the Colorado mountains.

As you rest by a blazing campfire outside the Last Dollar Hut and stare off across the canyon, you can't help but marvel at the grandness of the San Juans. Now nearly eye level with these surrounding 14,000-foot peaks, you also can't help but marvel at the strength it took to reach this point in your own journey. Make sure you return from your reverie before too long, as another day awaits.

Miles and Directions

0.0 START from the Coonskin parking lot in downtown Telluride. Bear left onto Mahoney Drive and again onto Colorado

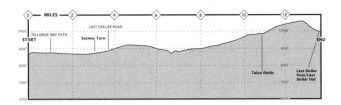

Avenue, riding west out of town. Intercept the paved Telluride Bicycle Path and ride to Society Turn.

3.0 Reach the intersection of Telluride Bicycle Path and Last Dollar Road by Society Turn. Cross Colorado Highway 145 and bear right onto Last Dollar Road (Forest Road 638).

5.1 Reach the intersection of the airport road and Last Dollar Road. Bear right at the top of the airport road (with the runway and hangers in sight to the left) onto the now dirt Last Dollar Road. A national forest access sign and a stop sign (facing the opposite direction) mark this intersection.

10.7 Enter the Uncompahgre National Forest.

11.2 Cross a talus field and continue riding through the aspen.

11.4 Cross another talus field.

12.8 Pass an old homestead to your left. Before crossing Summit Creek, a spring with water pouring from a black hose will be on your right. (As a general rule, avoid drinking from any unknown source of water, particularly in areas rich with mining and livestock grazing histories.) Begin climbing switchbacks as you near the final approach to the hut.

13.3 Reach Last Dollar Pass. Bear right at the crest, following the steep and rocky road at the edge of the trees, and hike-a-bike the last 0.25 mile up the ridge, to the east. (Don't follow the road that darts left into the forest.) You'll be able to see the hut when you're within 50 feet of it.

13.7 Arrive at the Last Dollar Hut.

Day 2 Last Dollar Hut to Spring Creek Hut

Starting with a massive loss in elevation, this day's ride is perhaps the easiest of the tour. The ruddy complexion of Hastings Mesa offers a bit of insight into the kind of landscape into which you're heading (the lunar-scaped terrain of Moab, Utah), while the grandness of Howard Flats recalls visions of the galloping ponies Ute Indians once raced there. After arriving at the Spring Creek Hut, riders can include some sideline riding on Spring Creek Trail 116. Spring Creek Trail 116 features some of the Uncompahgre Plateau's best singletrack. The 12-mile (one way) Spring Creek Trail 116 passes through meadows, aspen groves, and creeks. Consult with the San Juan Hut System for more information.

Start: From the Last Dollar Hut.

Distance: 27 miles.

Approximate riding time: Advanced riders, 2 to 3 hours; intermediate riders, 3 to 4 hours.

Technical difficulty: Technically easy due to the well-maintained dirt roads.

Physical difficulty: Physically easy to moderate due to the long descent from the Last Dollar Hut. What moderate ascending there is comes at the end of the ride.

Terrain: Well-maintained dirt road and 1 mile of paved road. Aside from a fast, sometimes loose, rocky descent from the Last Dollar Hut, the route to the Spring Creek Hut travels mostly through flat meadows, large valleys, and expansive plateaus.

Nearest town: Montrose, Colorado.

Other trail users: Sightseers, hunters, hikers, campers, and picnickers.

Spring Creek Hut.

The Ride

The second day of your escape has all the makings of a fast getaway, as you speedily descend to the paved Colorado Highway 62 before eventually intersecting with Howard Flats. Day two marks the beginning of your two-and-one-half-day tour of the Uncompahgre Plateau, where Ute Indians once thrived. From Last Dollar Hut, continue riding on Last Dollar Road to CO 62. En route, you'll descend through a forest of mixed aspens and conifers, passing old homesteads and paralleling Hastings Mesa. Once atop Hastings Mesa, you're treated to views of the Mount Sneffels Wilderness, including 14,150-foot Mount Sneffels. After intersecting CO 62 (the road that joins Placerville, in the southwest, with Dallas Divide and Ridgway, in the northeast), bear left onto CO

62 and speed down the paved road. If you were to bear right onto CO 62, you'd soon reach the top of Dallas Divide and the town of Ridgway, which is perhaps next on Colorado's ever-dwindling list of mountain towns on the brink of massive discovery. Peter R. Decker's *Old Fences, New Neighbors* (University of Arizona Press, Tucson, 1998) eloquently details Ridgway's burgeoning popularity.

After turning right off CO 62, you ride up Buck Canyon and onto Howard Flats. Howard Flats used to be an old Ute horse-racing track. Aside from its recreational use, the horse proved a formidable addition to the Utes' culture. Before the Spanish brought horses into North America, the Utes had led a primarily leaderless and wandering existence. With the arrival of the horse, the Utes began to redefine themselves. They became individual, chief-led bands of hunters and warriors. They were also among the first tribes to maintain extensive domesticated horse herds. More horses meant more Ute Indians could hunt and raid with greater speed and ease. Ute hunters gradually perfected their economy of motion. They would blitz into enemy Comanche-Arapaho territory and kill as many bison as they could, and still manage to make it back to their camps within half a moon's time (roughly fifteen days). The efficiency with which Utes could now travel enabled braves standing watch to react to enemy attacks with lightning speed. With their improved response, life inside Ute camps became more relaxed.

Horse racing became one of the Utes' most beloved pastimes. Whenever there was a social occasion, whether a wedding or a dance or a powwow, there was horse racing. The race became so much a part of Ute life that no camp was complete without its own racetrack. Before there was a

Day 2 Last Dollar Hut to Spring Creek Hut

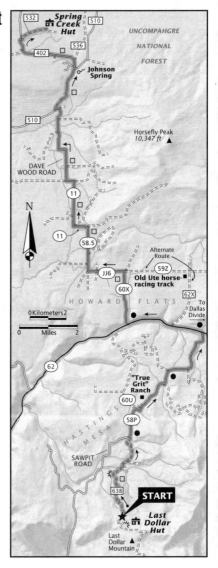

Denver or an INVESCO field at Mile High, there was Howard Flats, home to the original big league broncos. If viewed from above, the Flats show long, straight sections of hoof-trodden earth, pinpointing the precise location where these races were held. Gambling eventually found its way into horse racing, and the scene began to spread, now starting to include white settlers. It was horse racing that would prove to be the gateway to a life of crime for men such as Butch Cassidy and his gang.

Cassidy first met Matt Warner, already an accomplished cattle rustler and horse racer, while at a horse race in Telluride in 1885. The young Cassidy, who worked as an ore hauler for one of the area mines, took a liking to Warner—despite the fact that Cassidy had lost his savings to Warner in horse-racing debts. And Warner, in turn, liked Cassidy, if for no other reason than that Cassidy kept him in business. The two eventually became partners in their own horse-racing business.

With their best horse, Betty, and others like her, Butch and Matt managed to beat every horse in southern Colorado and Utah. While racing in Cortez, Matt met up with his brother-in-law Tom McCarty and invited him to join in their racing business. The three of them set out to become the area's most successful horse-racing team. Butch, Matt, and Tom made names for themselves throughout the racing circuit of southern Colorado and Utah, so much so that, in time, only Indians would race against them.

At one such race, an Indian, who had lost his pony and a stack of blankets to the three men, launched a barrage of insults and threats, objecting to their win. Having been so affronted, Tom beat the Indian with a rawhide riding whip.

The three quickly bolted from the scene to Tom's cabin. The next morning, Butch, Matt, and Tom awoke to the shrill cries of Indians. The Indians approached the cabin and demanded the return of their pony. When one of the Indians pointed a rifle at Tom, Tom quickly reacted, shooting the Indian off his horse, effectively ending the discussion.

From Howard Flats, you ride silently on, brooding over the possibility of a ghost encounter with an angry Indian. Once beyond the Flats, you begin your two-and-one-half-day journey across the Uncompahgre Plateau, Ute domain.

Miles and Directions

0.0 START from the Last Dollar Hut. Bear left from the front door and walk (reducing further trail damage) your bicycle down the path located to the north side of the hut. This is not the way you came. When the path widens enough to allow a truck's passing, begin riding and descend from the pass on Last Dollar Road.

0.4 Reach the intersection of the path and Last Dollar Road (Forest Road 638). Bear right onto Last Dollar Road and descend the north side of Last Dollar Mountain.

1.7 Arrive at a beautiful vista, on your left, with views of Hastings Mesa to the north, Wilson Peak to the south, and the La Sal Mountains to the distant west.

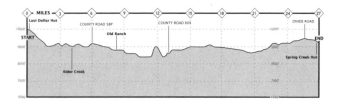

4.4 After crossing two cattle guards, cross Alder Creek. Climb from Alder Creek onto Hastings Mesa and intersect County Road 58P.

6.0 Reach the intersection of Last Dollar Road, Sawpit Road, and CR 58P. Bear right onto CR 58P.

8.4 Near San Juan Vista, pass an old ranch to the left. (This ranch was in the John Wayne movie *True Grit.*)

11.1 County Road 58P intersects with paved Colorado Highway 62 at a stop sign. Bear left onto CO 62 and descend on pavement to CR 60X, passing CR 62X on the right. **Option:** For a more remote route in dry conditions, the San Juan Hut System recommends turning right onto CR 62X and following this to CR 59Z. Turn left onto CR 59Z. This is the Price Canyon route. Pick up the directions at Mile 18.7 below.

13.8 Reach the intersection of CO 62 and CR 60X. Bear right onto CR 60X, by an old ski cabin on the left. Begin climbing, moderately, up Buck Canyon into Howard Flats, site of an old Ute Indian horse-racing track.

17.2 Pass an old homestead, seen through a wide valley to your left.

18.7 Reach the intersection of CR JJ6 and CR 59Z, by the San Juan Ranch gate and sign. Bear left onto CR JJ6.

19.1 County Road JJ6 will turn into CR 58.5 at a right curve. Bear right, continuing on CR 58.5.

20.8 County Road 58.5 connects with CR 11. Bear left onto CR 11.

21.0 County Road 11 intersects with Dave Wood Road. Bear right onto Dave Wood Road, passing under power lines and descending moderately into a large valley.

23.9 Reach the intersection of Sanborn Park Road (marked by a Sanborn Park sign) and Dave Wood Road. Bear right, continuing on Dave Wood Road, past the sign for Montrose. From here, the next and final 3 miles make up one long, steady climb to the Spring Creek Hut.

24.6 Enter the Uncompahgre National Forest.

25.5 Pass Johnson Spring on your right. This spring, fenced in by split aspen logs, features potable water pouring from a black hose.

25.6 Reach the intersection of Dave Wood Road and Divide Road. A sign reads COLUMBINE PASS, 31 MILES. Bear left here onto Divide Road (FR 402).

25.9 Reach the intersection of Divide Road and Spring Creek Rim Road. Bear right onto Spring Creek Rim Road where you will cross three cattle guards before turning left onto the path leading to the Spring Creek Hut.

26.1 Cross the first cattle guard.

26.4 Cross the second cattle guard.

26.8 Cross the third cattle guard.

27.0 Bear left, after a large water bar ditch, onto a path leading into the woods. An enormous cut section of a Douglas fir trunk lies to the left of the path. Follow this short path to the Spring Creek Hut.

27.0 Arrive at the Spring Creek Hut.

Day 3 Spring Creek Hut to Columbine Hut

Day three offers a pleasurably mellow cruise atop the Uncompahgre Plateau, traveling over gently rolling terrain on Divide Road, the major southeast-to-northwest thoroughfare across the Plateau. Divide Road is thickly lined with old-growth evergreen forests, lending the riding an air of peaceful solitude. Although the trees enclose most of the trail, there are three dramatic overlooks, evenly spaced along the route, which demand attention.

Start: From the Spring Creek Hut.

Distance: 34.8 miles.

Approximate riding time: Advanced riders, 3 to 3.5 hours; intermediate riders, 4 to 5 hours.

Technical difficulty: Technically easy. The route follows atop the relatively flat Uncompahgre Plateau via the well-maintained Divide Road.

Physical difficulty: Physically easy due to the minimal elevation gain.

Terrain: Improved dirt road. The Uncompahgre Plateau offers a relatively flat but densely forested ride.

Nearest town: Montrose, Colorado.

Other trail users: Anglers, hikers, hunters, and campers.

Alternate singletrack route: Approximately 45 miles. A parallel singletrack route can be ridden along all or part of this section with easy bailout options back to the standard route detailed in this chapter. Contact the San Juan Hut System for details.

The Ride

The third leg of the journey travels through the heart of the Uncompahgre Plateau, summiting it atop Columbine Pass. From the Spring Creek Hut, the riding on Divide Road features densely forested terrain. The day's riding is marked more by a sense of quiet solitude than by mind-blowing views. That's not to say there are no views; quite the contrary. The first of three incredible overlooks is at 5.7 miles, the Uncompahgre Overlook. To the east lie the peaks of Wetterhorn and Uncompahgre.

Wetterhorn Peak resembles a shark's nose. Named by the Wheeler Survey Team in 1874, the peak undoubtedly takes its name from the Swiss mountain of the same name, but finding a resemblance to the Swiss behemoth might require a bit of imagination. Just to the south of Wetterhorn Peak lies the Henson Creek Valley, a hotbed of mining activity. The chief city in the valley was Capitol City (established in the mid-1870s). Its misleading name was purely intentional. George T. Lee, Capitol City founder and owner of the town's main economic draw, the Lee Mining and Smelting Company, had visions of relocating Colorado's capital to Capitol City. His scheme was so elaborate as to include building a two-story brick house, later dubbed "the Governor's Mansion," with bricks imported from Pueblo. Lee's capital dreams would eventually dissolve after silver prices dropped in 1893.

To the east of Wetterhorn Peak lies Uncompahgre Peak, the largest in the San Juan Range. Towering over the Cimarron River and Big Blue Creek drainage, Uncompahgre Peak is one of the San Juan's most prominent landmarks. The word "uncompahgre" (pronounced "oon-cum-pa-gray")

Sitting out a rain and hail storm.

comes from the Shoshonean language, a dialect of the Uto-Aztecan language, and means "hot [unca] water [pah] spring [gre]." The Ute Indians found this San Juan precipice an ideal lookout. The name was officially given by the Hayden Survey Team during the latter part of the 1800s.

During a massive study of the San Juans, Hayden Survey members A. D. Wilson and Franklin Rhoda made the first documented ascent of the peak in the summer of 1874. Once atop the peak, the two noticed markings in the ground. The markings turned out to be grizzly paw prints. Evidently, the area surrounding Uncompahgre Peak was a favorite haunt among grizzlies. Given this, it seems no surprise that the Utes would convene here, as they held the bear in high regard, so much so that they called their most sacred and popular spring dance the Bear Dance. With thoughts of dancing bears aside, riders press on past the Uncompahgre Overlook to the Mount Sneffels Overlook.

The Mount Sneffels Overlook is at 10.3 miles into your ride. Mount Sneffels has been dubbed "Queen of the San Juans." It is one of those hallmark precipices that can hypnotize an observer for hours. Below this royal peak, reflecting its lofty throne, is the Blue Lakes Basin. During the Hayden Survey of 1874, a member of the team remarked that the basin reminded him of the absorbing hole described in Jules Verne's *Journey to the Center of the Earth*. Alluding to the Icelandic mountain located near the "hole" in Verne's novel, survey member Dr. Endlich exclaimed, "There's Snaefell," which in Icelandic means "snowfield." Today we have sufficiently corrupted the spelling and pronunciation to give us Mount Sneffels.

Just under a mile from Columbine Pass and the top of the Uncompahgre Plateau, riders are offered their third and most dramatic scenic overlook: the Tabeguache Overlook, with views of the Dolores River Valley to the west. The Tabeguache (meaning "sunny side") were a band of Ute Indians who lived in the valleys of the Gunnison and Uncompahgre Rivers. They lived in harmony with their natural surroundings. Of all the Tabeguache, perhaps no one was more prominent than Chief Shavano. The chief worked closely with Chief Ouray, leader of the Ute Nation, to help establish peaceful relations between the whites and the Utes. Chief Shavano's leadership was such that Chief Ouray, perhaps the greatest of all Ute chiefs, favored him as his successor. As a tribute to his tireless efforts to bring about peace, Chief Shavano is one of only four Indians to have a Colorado Fourteener bear his name: Mount Shavano (14,229

Day 3 Spring Creek Hut to Columbine Hut

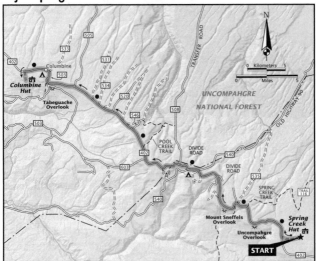

feet). Today, descendants of the Tabeguache, along with members of the Grand, Yampa, and Uintah bands, constitute the Northern Utes. They live on the Uintah-Ouray Reservation, with their headquarters in Fort Duchesne, Utah.

From the Tabeguache Overlook, riders pass over Columbine Pass (where potable water is available) and continue in the direction of Windy Point, before arriving at the Columbine Hut.

Miles and Directions

0.0   START from the Spring Creek Hut. Ride up the path back to Spring Creek Rim Road. Bear right onto Spring Creek Rim Road, heading back toward Divide Road.

0.2   Cross the first cattle guard.

0.6   Cross the second cattle guard.

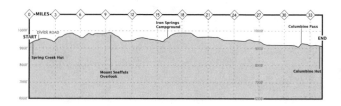

0.9 Cross the third cattle guard.

1.1 Reach the intersection of Spring Creek Rim Road and Divide Road (Forest Road 402). Bear right (north) onto Divide Road, toward Columbine Pass.

5.7 Reach the Uncompahgre Overlook, to your left. There are views of Precipice Peak (13,144 feet), Uncompahgre Peak (14,309 feet), and Wetterhorn Peak (14,015 feet).

8.3 Reach the intersection of Divide Road and the Spring Creek Trail, the Uncompahgre Plateau's premier singletrack. Continue riding on Divide Road.

10.3 Mount Sneffels Overlook is to your left. There are views of Mount Sneffels (14,150 feet), Lizard Head (13,113 feet), Wilson Peak (14,017 feet), and Mount Wilson (14,246 feet).

15.6 Reach the intersection of Divide Road and Old Colorado Highway 90 (FR 540). Old Highway 90 will be to your right. Continue on Divide Road, following signs for Columbine Pass.

16.1 Pass Iron Springs Campground, on your left.

17.3 The intersection for Transfer Road and FR 27 will be to your right, as you continue riding on Divide Road.

18.8 Pass West Antone Springs 559, to your left.

19.9 Pass Pool Creek Trail 113, to your right.

20.6 Pass Delta/Nucla Road, to your left.

23.4 Pass East Bull Creek, to your right.

Taking in the views.

31.7 Tabeguache Overlook is on your left.

32.5 Reach Columbine Pass and bear right onto FR 503.

33.3 Reach Columbine Campground. Toilet facilities are available. Good drinking water is available from the spring.

33.7 Arrive at the intersection of FR 402 and FR 503. Bear left (west), following FR 402 (still Divide Road) toward Windy Point.

34.5 Pass a dirt road leading off to the left.

34.7 Bear left onto this second dirt road leading into the woods. Follow this small, non-gravel road for roughly 200 yards to the hut.

34.8 Arrive at the Columbine Hut.

Day 4 Columbine Hut to Graham Ranch Cabin

Day four is perhaps the journey's most spectacular leg. As you near the end of your two-and-one-half-day tour of the Uncompahgre Plateau, you ride down the western edge of the plateau over the rolling Divide Road. En route, vertigo-inducing views of the La Sal Mountains and the high deserts of southeastern Utah mesmerize your visual senses. Fear not the hypnotic trance in which you may find yourself. Let it carry you through to the Graham Ranch Cabin. A turn-of-the-century rancher's cabin and a working cow camp, Graham Ranch Cabin is constructed of notched logs chinked with mortar. Poised among quaking aspens in a far corner of the Craig Ranch, overlooking a horse corral, Graham Ranch's idyllic setting only serves to enhance the buzz already acquired from the day's view-tiful ride.

Start: From the Columbine Hut.
Distance: 36.9 miles.
Approximate riding time: Advanced riders, 2.5 to 3 hours; intermediate riders, 3.5 to 4 hours.
Technical difficulty: Technically easy due to traveling on mildly undulating terrain, along the well-maintained Divide Road.
Physical difficulty: Physically easy due to the moderately level route along the well-maintained Divide Road.
Terrain: Improved dirt road. The route travels atop the densely forested Uncompahgre Plateau, with open views as you near the plateau's western edge.
Nearest town: Gateway, Colorado.
Other trail users: Hikers, hunters, campers, anglers, and sightseers.

Graham Ranch Cabin and bikes.

The Ride

For two and one-half days you've been riding on the Uncompahgre Plateau. Day four marks the final leg of your travels on Divide Road and the plateau. But what exactly is this Uncompahgre Plateau, and where does it fit in the grand scheme of things? Unlike the San Juan Mountains, whose high-alpine peaks were formed ten to forty million years ago by volcanic upheaval and glaciation, the Uncompahgre Plateau was formed by a series of massive uplifts caused by internal disturbances of the Earth's crust. Mysteriously the Uncompahgre Plateau somehow escaped the geological turmoil that swept across the West to form the Sierra Nevadas, the ranges of Nevada and Utah, and the Rocky Mountains.

The Uncompahgre Plateau is located on the Colorado Plateau Province's eastern border. This province encompasses the vast area of flat-lying sedimentary rock extending into Utah, Arizona, and New Mexico. The Uncompahgre Plateau stretches in a southeast-to-northwest direction from the San Juan Mountains to the Utah border southwest of Grand Junction. A virtually flat mesa stretching 25 by 100 miles, the plateau, when viewed from a distance, is far less striking than its neighboring San Juan and West Elk Mountains. Because it pales by comparison, the plateau has achieved a certain degree of anonymity. Nevertheless, the Uncompahgre Plateau is, indeed, part of the ancestral Rocky Mountains and deserves attention. Its existence stems from the Uncompahgria uplift, the ancient range lifted high by faulting about 300 million years ago. A series of lesser uplifts, occurring roughly one million years ago, gave the plateau its present formation.

▶ **For further reading:** *Uncompahgre: A Guide to the Uncompahgre Plateau,* by Muriel Marshall, Valley Books, 3rd edition, 1998; 328 East Main Street, Montrose, CO, 81401; (970) 249-1841.

Although archaeological evidence suggests that people have been living on the Uncompahgre Plateau for at least 10,000 years, its recorded history did not start until the late 1770s. In 1776 two Spanish priests, Silvestre Velez de Escalante and Francisco Antanasio Dominguez, accompanied by a Ute guide, led a party from Sante Fe, New Mexico, across the Uncompahgre Plateau in search of safe passage

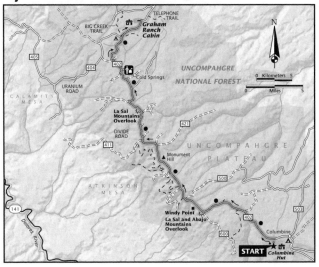

to the missions of California. As winter approached, the two decided to call off their search and head back to Santa Fe.

Fifty-two years later, Antoine Robidoux, who had been operating a fur trapper supply business in St. Louis, Missouri, built a trading post near the present town of Delta, Colorado. In response to the popularity of the top hat (which was made of beaver pelts), many trappers flocked to the Uncompahgre in search of beaver. Robidoux's Fort Uncompahgre, functioning as a supply station for trappers and Indians alike, became a meeting ground for these two very different peoples. The fort was significant in that it provided an arena where trappers and Indians would meet; these two groups would seldom see each other outside of the trading room. Fort Uncompahgre was also significant in that it was one of only two white settlements in all of Colorado. This would change, however, when in 1850 the United States laid claim to all of western Colorado.

In 1853 Congress ordered Captain John Gunnison to explore the new territory and report on its potential. His travels took him from the Great Plains to the San Luis Valley, over Cochetopa Pass, down the Gunnison River, and into the Uncompahgre Valley. Gunnison would happen upon the ruins of Fort Uncompahgre, which had been set ablaze by Ute Indians shortly after it was built. Gunnison wrote of a savage and rugged Colorado, one that did not sound entirely hospitable. But to his credit, he did detail information that proved particularly helpful in future expeditions, like the Wheeler and Hayden surveys.

Wheeler and Hayden discovered the San Juan Mountains and the Uncompahgre Plateau to be rife with minerals. Once the news of this got out, countless miners and prospectors flocked to the mountains to set up shop. As the mountain mining increased, resident Utes were pushed farther and farther from their settlements. The mushrooming mining towns became the economic, social, and political lifeline of the Uncompahgre country and paved the way for other industries to move in. By the 1880s it was no surprise when tens of thousands of cattle were grazing on the plateau. The large number of cattle, coupled with loose grazing regulations, eventually turned many large tracts into barren wastelands. This resulted in the turn-of-the-century establishment of federal land reserves, precursors to our national forests.

As you ride the former chuckwagon trail of the Divide Road, dodging perhaps ten cattle, instead of tens of thousands, you can't help but appreciate our national forest system. That appreciation comes fully to bear when you arrive at Windy Point. Here the dramatic upward arching of the plateau's rock layers is brought into view, as the plateau itself drops precipitously nearly 2,000 feet in a collection of cliffs and slopes to Burro Creek. Looking northwest from Windy Point, you're offered a unique bird's-eye view of the plateau's abrupt west face. A pair of eagles can often be seen soaring high above the cliffs.

But eagles aren't the only birds to take up permanent residence on the plateau. Located just after the turnoff leading to the Graham Ranch Cabin lies the nearby Telephone Trail, so called for the variety of nesting holes bored in the trail's tree trunks. Telephone Trail makes for a great wind-down hike after you settle in at the cabin. The entire trail courses through a cavity-nesting bird habitat that's noted for its variety of uncommon birds that nest in holes burrowed into standing dead trees. Northern pygmy-owls *(Glancidium gnoma),* flammulated owls *(Otus flammeolus),* hairy woodpeckers *(Picoides villosus),* nuthatches *(Sitta canadensis* and *Sitta carolinensis),* and swallows *(Tachycineta thalassina)* all may be seen while hiking. If hiking after biking isn't your style, simply chill out at the cabin, a hideout with real character.

Miles and Directions

0.0 START from the Columbine Hut and backtrack to Divide Road (Forest Road 402).

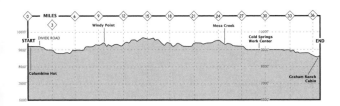

0.1	Intersect with Divide Road. Bear left (north) onto Divide Road and start riding toward Windy Point.
9.4	Reach Windy Point. A scenic overlook of the La Sal and Abajo (Blue) Mountains faces west.
13.0	You're offered the first view of the Grand Mesa, to your right (northeast), near the town of Grand Junction.
13.9	Leave Montrose County and enter Mesa County.
22.3	Pass Uncompahgre Butte (9,732 feet), to your right.
23.2	The La Sal Mountains vista is to the west.
25.2	Pass Mesa Creek, to the left.
27.6	To the northeast lies the largest view of the Grand Mesa.
29.1	Pass the ranger station and the Cold Springs Work Center, on your right.
33.3	Pass the Divide Forks Campground, on your left.
33.5	Reach the junction of Divide Road (FR 402) and Uranium Road (FR 404). Continue straight (right) on Divide Road toward Grand Junction.
33.7	Pass Big Creek Trail 656, on your left. (Note: The U.S. Forest Service has closed Big Creek Trail to bikes.)
36.6	Reach the intersection of Divide Road and the doubletrack on the left, which leads to the cabin. Bear left onto this doubletrack (which bears the sign PRIVATE ACCESS ROAD) directly before the cattle guard that crosses Divide Road. Follow the split-rail fence (which eventually turns into a barbed wire fence) to the cabin. Telephone Trail begins to the right, just over the cattle guard.
36.9	Arrive at the Graham Ranch Cabin.

Day 5 **Graham Ranch Cabin to Gateway Hut**

Along with the mostly descending, 9-mile stretch of single-track of Ute Creek Trail 608, on this section riders are treated to great views of the La Sal Mountains and the canyons of the Dolores River Valley. From the cool forests atop the western flank of the Uncompahgre Plateau, riders also descend along a 6-mile shelf into the sandstone canyons of the Dolores River Valley/West Creek. In total, the ride drops you 4,900 feet from the Graham Ranch Cabin to the Gateway Hut. The Gateway Hut is located in the tiny town of Gateway, Colorado. Unless you brought it with you, you've had no access to adult beverages in over four days. The Gateway Tavern can help. But take note: It's closed on Mondays, so plan your trip accordingly.

Start: From the Graham Ranch Cabin.

Distance: 28 miles.

Approximate riding time: Advanced riders, 2.5 to 3 hours; intermediate riders, 3 to 4 hours.

Technical difficulty: Technically easy to challenging. Most of this leg travels over well-maintained dirt road; however, the optional singletrack spur involves steep, rocky descents along sand and dirt-packed trail. Also, there's a pulse-racing descent over rocky road from the top of the Uncompahgre Plateau into the Dolores River Valley.

Physical difficulty: Physically easy to moderate. The intermittent short, but tough, climbs of the singletrack spur, coupled with the more moderate climbs along the road, make this leg of the journey moderately physical.

Terrain: Improved dirt road, paved state highway, doubletrack, and singletrack. Near the western edge of the plateau, the thick, forested terrain gives way to rockier and sandier, semiarid terrain. Sand and exposed rocks and roots are all to be expected along this route, particularly on the singletrack spur. As you enter into the Dolores River Valley and a flash flood zone, there are large sections of deep sand.

Nearest town: Gateway, Colorado.

Other trail users: Hikers, campers, four-wheelers, hunters, and sightseers.

Alternate singletrack route: This day has tremendous singletrack options, of which the Ute Creek Trail, featured on the map, is one. Contact the San Juan Hut System for more details.

The Ride

From the Graham Ranch Cabin, riders return to Divide Road and backtrack to its intersection with Uranium Road. As its name suggests, Uranium Road was once used to transport uranium from the many plateau mines. Uranium was being shipped to Grand Junction as early as World War I, where it was used to aid in the war effort. Uranium Road follows an old Ute trail that the Indians used frequently. This old Ute trail will eventually connect with one of the day's highlights, the singletrack of the aptly named Ute Creek Trail 608.

Ute Creek Trail is an optional singletrack spur from the main route, but one well worth taking. The trail descends through thick aspens, over big rock drop-offs, into chilling creek beds, across sweeping meadows, and through piñon-juniper forests before letting out onto slickrock and sandstone. At 9.4 miles the views of the La Sal Mountains and John Brown Canyon are engulfing. Adding to the challenge of the singletrack is the extra weight that bike touring

Doing a balancing act with the La Sal Mountains beyond.

necessitates. Panniers might be the way to go when touring on well-maintained forest roads, but their value is called into question when barreling down tight and rocky singletrack. The extra weight adds a new dimension to singletrack riding. After you intersect with Snowshoe Trail, it's a short grunt of a climb to Pine Mountain Road.

After riding roughly 1.5 miles from this intersection, the route unfolds to an overwhelming view of the Dolores River Valley/West Creek. From the western flank of the Uncompahgre Plateau, you descend abruptly along a shelf road into the valley—a valley consisting of a maze of mesas and canyons. This is a hair-raising section of the ride. The shelf falls steeply from the plateau with nothing to your right save a 300-foot drop to the canyon floor. This marks the

Day 5 Graham Ranch Cabin to Gateway Hut

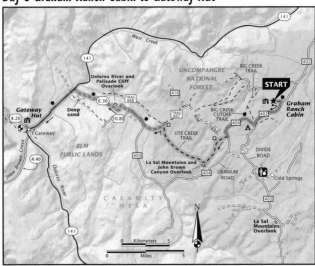

beginning of a fast and furious descent into the Dolores River Valley and the town of Gateway.

The Dolores River received its name from the Spanish missionaries Dominguez and Escalante, who, in 1776, led an expedition across the Uncompahgre Plateau in search of safe passage to the missions of California. To reach the Ute Trail (Uranium Road), which crossed over the Uncompahgre Plateau, the expedition had to ford the then unnamed Dolores River. After realizing that they had passed the point where they should have crossed the river, Dominguez and Escalante hastily ordered their expedition to cross where they were. This decision proved costly, since Dominguez, Escalante, and their expedition found themselves entangled in thorny brush and standing before a steep canyon wall. They struggled to scale the wall to the top of the plateau, so much so that their horses' hooves started to bleed. Having endured such great pain and suffering in the crossing, the priests consequently named the river, appropriately enough, "dolores" or "pains."

In the 1880s gold was discovered on Mesa Creek Flats, located upriver, just 4 miles below the junction of the Dolores River and the San Miguel River. Soon thereafter prospectors were panning for gold in Mesa Creek. However there was one slight hitch to this endeavor: Gold panning was limited to only the spring and early summer, since water flow from Mesa Creek was quite small. By midsummer, in fact, Mesa Creek would run dry, effectively putting an end to gold panning in Mesa Creek Flats until the winter's snowmelt would again give rise to Mesa Creek. These circumstances inspired the Montrose Placer Mining Company, managed by Colonel N. P. Turner, to construct the San Miguel Flume, one of Colorado's greatest engineering achievements. The mining company believed that if enough water were to rush through Mesa Creek and into the flats, millions of dollars' worth of gold could be recovered from the soil all year through. Construction on the flume began in 1889 and was completed two years later. In 1891 this ambitious project began diverting water from the San Miguel River to Mesa Creek, a distance of roughly 12 miles.

Turner's intent was to mine Mesa Creek hydraulically, using pressurized water to sift the heavier gold particles from the river sediment. The water and sediment mixture would flow through a sluice box and over a riffle board. The sluice, which closely resembles a flume, was angled to allow the mixture to sift through. The riffles were small slats that ran perpendicular to the sides of the sluice box, much like venetian blinds might look if lain open in a shoebox. The riffles would catch the sand containing the heavier gold particles.

Turner's diversion plan called for an 8-mile-long, 4-foot-deep, and 6-foot-wide flume running along the northern wall of the San Miguel Canyon. Workers were literally hung over the canyon wall, 250 to 500 feet below the rim and 100 to 150 feet above the riverbed, all in order to secure the flume into the sandstone walls. Once completed, the flume ran 1.5 miles on the sandstone cliffs above the San Miguel River and 6.5 miles on the canyon wall above the Dolores River. An estimated 1.8 million board-feet of lumber was used to construct the flume, which cost over $100,000 to build. The flume was an engineering success and worked beautifully, delivering more than eighty million gallons of water a day. But its true success was yet to be tested. Would it yield gold?

The gold found along the Mesa Creek Flats was known as "leaf gold," or "flour gold," consisting of a very fine powder. Because of the gold's fine consistency, it washed straight through the sluice. Remaining suspended in the water, the gold flushed directly over the riffles in the flume, in effect rendering them useless. It didn't take long for Turner, along with the Montrose Placer Mining Company stockholders, to realize that the entire project was a failure. With the entire investment in the flume lost, Turner became so dejected that he traveled to Chicago, rented a room, and shot himself in the head. After Turner's horrific demise, the flume was soon

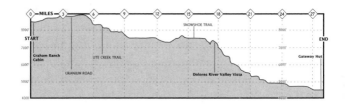

abandoned, left only to the scavenging ranchers whose cabins, sheds, and fences needed mending. Remnants of the flume still cling to sections of the canyon, near Uravan, roughly 25 miles south of Gateway.

Miles and Directions

0.0   START from the Graham Ranch Cabin and ride back up the doubletrack to Divide Road (Forest Road 402).

0.3   Reach the intersection of the doubletrack and Divide Road (FR 402). Bear right onto Divide Road (FR 402), and return to the intersection of Divide Road (FR 402) and Uranium Road (FR 404).

3.2   Pass Big Creek Trail, on your right. (Note: The U.S. Forest Service has closed Big Creek Trail to bikes.)

3.4   Reach the junction of Divide Road (FR 402) and Uranium Road (FR 404). Bear right onto Uranium Road (FR 404) and ride in a northwesterly direction.

4.6   Pass the Big Creek Cutoff Trail, to your right.

6.3   Pass Rim Trail (WOLF HILL—2 and BIG POND—3), to your right.

6.7   Reach the intersection of Uranium Road and Ute Creek Trail 608. Bear right onto Ute Creek Trail. **Option:** For those not interested in riding the singletrack, you can continue on Uranium Road for roughly 14.6 miles to the intersection of Uranium Road and County Road 6.30/FR 405. At a sign marking the turnoff to the town of Gateway, bear right onto CR 6.30/FR 405 and descend to Indian Creek. Continue on CR 6.30/FR 405 at all other intersections and ride for roughly 6.5 miles to Calamity Basin. Rejoin the others at the Snowshoe Trailhead. For more information, contact the San Juan Hut System.

7.7   Descend the rocky singletrack and ride straight through an opening in a barbed wire fence.

8.5   The singletrack delivers a short but rocky and sandy climb. Continue straight, through some scrub oak.

9.4 Arrive at an incredible vista of the La Sal Mountains and John Brown Canyon. This is a great lunch spot and photo op.

10.2 Arrive at another fence. Continue straight, passing through an opening in the fence, in a westerly direction between two pine trees.

11.4 The singletrack turns into a doubletrack. Continue riding on the doubletrack, which is marked by iron fence posts, as it snakes its way through sage and scrub oak forests.

14.5 Reach the intersection of Ute Creek Trail 608 and Snowshoe Trail (Trail 607); there are no trail signs at this intersection. Bear left onto Snowshoe Trail, a rough-looking dirt road, and ride back to Pine Mountain Road and the main route.

15.6 Reach the intersection of Snowshoe Trail and CR 6.30/FR 405 (Pine Mountain Road). Bear right onto Pine Mountain Road.

17.2 Reach the junction of Pine Mountain Road and CR 10.80. A sign for the town of Gateway will be to your right. Continue straight here, descending along the steep and rocky Pine Mountain Road (CR 6.30) into the Dolores River Valley.

17.9 Descend to a cattle guard with a vista of the Dolores River Valley. Views of Palisade Cliff are offered.

21.3 Enter into a flash flood zone and patches of deep sand. Be extremely cautious here, especially in inclement weather.

23.1 Reach the intersection of Pine Mountain Road (CR 6.30) and Colorado Highway 141, by a stop sign. Bear left (west), onto the paved highway, and descend into Gateway.

27.1 Enter into Gateway and ride west through it.

27.6 Bear right onto dirt road, just before crossing the Dolores River via a steel bridge. Ride on this dirt road to the Gateway Hut, with the Dolores River to your left.

28.0 Arrive at the Gateway Hut.

Day 6 **Gateway Hut to La Sal Hut**

The route connecting the Gateway Hut with the La Sal Hut is probably the toughest leg of the entire journey. Although the initial climb through John Brown Canyon is the steepest of the day, it also comes at the beginning of the day, so riders get the toughest part of the ride over with first. The route crosses the Colorado border and enters Utah near a cow camp. Since summertime temperatures in Gateway may exceed one hundred degrees, it's strongly suggested that you get an early start on the day's riding, taking advantage of the morning's cooler temperatures and avoiding afternoon thunderstorms. The La Sal Hut is the San Juan Hut System's newest hut. It was previously a yurt, until a local black bear clawed through its canvas walls. Gateway sits at 4,600 feet, while the La Sal Hut sits at 8,400 feet. You can do the math; it's a tough climb.

Start: From the Gateway Hut.

Distance: 22.3 miles.

Approximate riding time: Advanced riders, 3 to 4 hours; intermediate riders, 5 to 6 hours.

Technical difficulty: Technically easy to moderate due to the route's well-maintained dirt roads. Some areas include washboard and sandy segments.

Physical difficulty: Physically challenging due to the hotter temperatures and the steep and long climb from the Dolores River Valley to the La Sal Mountains via John Brown Canyon.

Terrain: Paved highway and improved dirt road. The route is sandy and rocky in spots as it makes its way through John Brown Canyon. Once above the canyon, loose gravel roads, along with rutted and sandy sections, make the climb to the La Sal Hut tough.

Nearest town: Moab, Utah.

Other trail users: Ranchers and sightseers.

The Ride

From the Gateway Hut, you start climbing almost immediately. This is a potential flash flood area. Get an early start to avoid the heat and the potential afternoon thunderstorms that roll through here frequently. Flash floods have been known to rush through John Brown Canyon in almost biblical proportions. The route through John Brown Canyon is a sandy—rutted in spots—road that cuts laboriously through the sheer, red sandstone canyon walls on its way to the La Sal Mountains. Only John Brown Creek, its accompanying cottonwoods, and the late-rising canyon sun provide any kind of relief from this torturous climb. Overhead, an old telegraph line suggests that there's a story of men who came long before you.

During America's early push west, these lines of communication proved to be a settlement's only link to the rest of the country. And it wasn't until 1897 that the link came into being. Due to this area's rugged and remote location, it didn't experience the relatively early colonization that Utah's Great Basin experienced. By 1847 Salt Lake City had already been established, but the areas surrounding the La Sal Mountains would not see any kind of settlement until the latter part of the 1870s. Although Spanish, Mexican, and American expeditions had passed through these parts as early as the 1760s, this area was considered far too remote and rugged to warrant settlement. In fact the La Sal Mountains were one of the last areas in the continental United States to attract government explorers and survey teams.

For all intents and purposes, it wasn't until 1877, when gritty stockmen and their livestock first arrived in the area, that the La Sal Mountains were given much consideration.

Crossing the state line into Utah! Photo: Amy Hlawaty

The first settlers to stake their claim to the area's large min-
eral and grazing resources were William Granstaff, an African
American, and a French-Canadian trapper whose name has
escaped historical records. The two prospected, grew vegetables, and raised cattle. They also eagerly claimed substantial
portions of a major La Sal Mountains drainage. To the west
of these claims lies the Colorado River; to the south, the San
Juan River; to the north, the Grand River; and to the east,
Mesa Verde country. Granstaff grazed his cattle in the

drainage, which later became known as Negro Bill Canyon, the canyon paralleling Porcupine Rim in Moab, Utah. During the next five years, cattle ranchers continued their move into the La Sal region, establishing communities in Little Grand Valley (later to be renamed "Moab"), Little Castle Valley, and on the south side of the La Sals. These early communities remained isolated from one another.

It wasn't until 1897 that J. N. Corbin organized the area's first telephone company, bringing service to Moab. Some of the more remote areas surrounding the La Sal Mountains, however, would remain without telephone service well into the 1920s. Following Corbin's lead, the newly created La Sal National Forest Service played a pivotal role in establishing the lines of communication in southeastern Utah. The La Sal Forest Reserve joined President Theodore Roosevelt's forest reserves relatively late—it wasn't created until January 25, 1906, roughly one year before all "reserves" became known as "national forests." As a latecomer, the La Sal National Forest Service was eager to establish itself as a viable institution.

With 128,960 acres in Utah and 29,502 acres in Colorado, it was crucial that the La Sal National Forest have the telephone communications to conduct its business. Most important, the telephone lines would allow for speedy notification in case of fire. By 1910 phone lines ran through most of the La Sal National Forest, and phone service, in turn, was made available to area locals. With these phone lines in place, ranches and outlying settlements were now in contact with one another, paving the way for further settlement.

With old telegraph lines looming overhead, you can't help but feel, somehow, in touch with those who have traveled this road before. Heading up John Brown Canyon, you

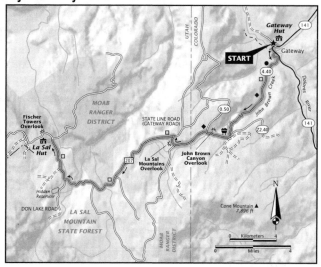

pass into an old uranium-mining area. Take care to stay on the main road and stay out of the dilapidated mines. These mines have a tendency to cave in and contain noxious and highly combustible gasses. Be thankful that your day's climbing is half over, with the steepest part of the climb behind you. Once you cross into Utah, the La Sal Mountains seemingly pop up from nowhere, looking curiously out of place.

Dubbed by early Spanish explorers as the "mountains of salt," the La Sals are, quite visibly, an island range. Though the range never erupted, the core began its life as a volcano. Over the years erosion crumpled away the softer, volcanic rock on the outside and revealed the cooled volcanic core on the inside. This cooled core subsequently solidified the remaining range. What had at one time been a volcano now remains exposed as the La Sal Mountains. With two prominent passes reaching over 10,000 feet, the La Sal Mountains are, indeed, no mere mounds of salt. The eleven peaks that make up the range have an average combined elevation of 11,930 feet. They are, from south to north: South Mountain (11,798 feet), Mount Tukuhnikivatz (12,483 feet), Mount Peale (12,721 feet), Mount Mellenthin (12,646 feet), Haystack Mountain (11,642 feet), Mount Tomasaki (12,230 feet), Manns Peak (12,273 feet), Gold Knob (11,055 feet), Mount Waas (12,331 feet), Horse Mountain (11,150 feet), and Grand View Mountain (10,905 feet). Their enormity only emphasizes the beauty of the mesas and valleys. The mountains, the mesas, and the valleys all make this one of the country's most striking landscapes.

Miles and Directions

0.0   Start from the Gateway Hut. Return the way you came to Colorado Highway 141.

0.4   Bear right onto CO 141, crossing the Dolores River. The road bends left and leads to a sign for John Brown Canyon.

0.9   Reach the junction of CO 141 and County Road 4.40. Bear right onto CR 4.40, after passing a sign for John Brown Canyon on the left, and cross a cattle guard.

1.4   The pavement ends. Here begins the climb through the steep and narrow-walled John Brown Canyon. (Be aware of the

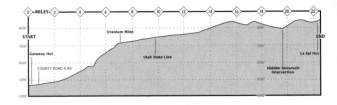

flash flood potential!) The road through the canyon is called alternately State Line Road or Gateway Road.

5.0 Begin to rise steeply out of the canyon.

7.1 Enter into the historic uranium-mining area. A warning sign marks your entrance. At this point you've already completed half of the day's climbing, and you begin to notice taller pine trees along the road.

7.2 Pass a BLM (Bureau of Land Management) sign and a road to your left. Continue straight.

8.0 Pass great views of John Brown Canyon, to your right.

8.6 Arrive at an intersection. Bear left here, by the Gateway sign.

9.8 Pass a cow camp in the valley, to your left, as you cross a cattle guard and the state line. Welcome to Utah.

15.4 Enter into the La Sal Mountain State Forest. Bypass the road on the left and continue heading straight for the mountains.

17.3 Arrive at a sign to your right reading 5 BAR A, KIRK'S BASIN—9, AND GATEWAY—16. Continue riding straight—do not bear left—as you continue to climb.

19.3 Pass a sign indicating that you are leaving the La Sal Mountain State Forest. There will be another sign for the Taylor Livestock Company.

19.7 Reach the Hidden Reservoir intersection by Don Lake Road and State Line Road. Pass Don Lake Road, to your left, and continue on State Line Road. **Option:** Bear left onto Don Lake Road at the sign for Don Lake and Beaver Basin to enjoy a refreshing dip in Hidden Reservoir. It's only a small diversion from the main route. To get to Hidden Reservoir: Travel along Don Lake Road for approximately 0.5 mile. Bear right, down the four-wheel-drive road, just before the first cattle guard you come to.

20.5 Pass the MANTI–LA SAL NATIONAL FOREST sign.

22.3 Bear left (west) onto the four-wheel-drive road leading into a dense oak thicket. (If you've reached a T intersection with a sign reading MOAB—38 and NORTH BEAVER MESA—4.5, you've gone too far. Turn around and backtrack roughly 500 feet south to the four-wheel-drive road, which will now be on your right.) Ride the four-wheel-drive road approximately 400 feet to the La Sal Hut.

Day 7 La Sal Hut to Moab

Your final push to the end, in a way, encapsulates your entire seven-day odyssey. From the high alpine forests of the La Sal Mountains, through the sage-piñon fields of Moab's higher plateaus and mesas, to the surreal slickrock and sandstone formations of Moab's canyonlands, you descend an eye-popping 5,700 feet through a veritable time capsule of natural history. The entire route overlooks western Colorado and eastern Utah, prominently displaying views of Fischer Valley, Fischer Towers, and Castle Valley. Although the main route of this final leg descends along Sand Flats Road into Moab, a worthwhile alternative would be to break from this road at 28.1 miles and connect with Porcupine Rim Trail, one of Moab's most incredible singletrack trails.

Start: From the La Sal Hut.
Distance: 38.4 miles.
Approximate riding time: Advanced riders, 3.5 to 4 hours; intermediate riders, 4 to 5 hours.
Technical difficulty: Technically moderate due to the variety of loose and exposed rocks, particularly on Sand Flats Road.
Physical difficulty: Physically moderate due to the hotter temperatures of Moab and the length of the climbs.

Terrain: Improved dirt road, four-wheel-drive road, and paved road. Slickrock and large, exposed, loose rock make up the majority of the terrain. Sand and roots fill in the gaps. The sand and rock may cause unsteadiness on the more heavily weighted bicycles.
Nearest town: Moab, Utah.
Other trail users: Hikers, sightseers, and four-wheelers.

Castleton Tower.

Getting there: From Moab, Utah: Drive south on Main Street (U.S. Highway 191) to 100 South Street. Turn right (west) onto 100 South Street (by the Arby's) and drive for a block and a half. Bear left into the municipal parking lot behind the police station and park your vehicle here.

The Ride

Moab, Utah, seems a fitting finale to this weeklong getaway. It's been host, holdup, and hideout to a number of western outlaws—none more notable than Tom McCarty. Perhaps more than any other bad boy, Tom McCarty helped solidify Moab's outlaw mystique. The McCarty family rode into town in the late 1870s. The McCartys were part of the vast migration of cattlemen and cowboys who were moving into southeastern Utah at the time. They were an independent lot, aggressive and adventurous. Of course, they had to be, given the area's unsettled terrain and remoteness. When the McCartys led their large herd of cattle across the Wasatch Mountains to roam in Moab's open ranges, no one thought to ask where they had gotten their cattle from; no one much cared.

Tom McCarty and his brother Bill operated their ranch near the La Sal Mountains. At the time, the ranch was situated on the best open range in Utah. Nevertheless, the two brothers sold it for $35,000 and turned, instead, to a life of crime. "My downfall commenced by gambling," Tom later wrote. "Horse racing was the first . . ." (see Day 2), followed by cattle rustling soon thereafter. From Moab, Tom took his cattle rustling on the road, traveling to Arizona, New Mexico, and Iowa.

While in Iowa he bought three of the fastest horses he could find. These horses would later provide transport for history's "Wild Bunch" (which included Butch Cassidy, Matt Warner, and, of course, Tom), as they made their getaway with $30,000 of Telluride's money (see Day 1). As leader of another thieving troupe, the "Blue Mountain Gang," Tom would go on robbing in Utah and, indeed, throughout a major part of the American West for another four years. Sometime in the mid- to late 1890s, Tom penned his autobiography and sent the manuscript to Matt Warner's father. Then he simply disappeared. *The History of Tom McCarty* was published in 1898.

With such notorious beginnings, it's ironic that Moab acquired its name from the Bible. In 1881 W. A. Pierce, an avid Bible-reader (and minority by association thereof), gave the town its present name. Pierce recalled the stories of the "Far Country," a region distinguished for its remoteness and its flat-topped plateaus. This description of the biblical "Moab" closely resembled what he saw in Moab, Utah. Given what we know of Moab's raucous past, the name seems a fittingly formidable-sounding replacement for the town's previous name. "Little Grand Canyon" just doesn't have the punch Moab has; it's too contradictory to stand for that bold and independent town into which we now ride.

We ride into these canyonland badlands following the outlaw trail. High in the La Sal Mountains, we reach the Castle Valley Overlook at 9.3 miles. Here one can view Castleton Tower, Castle Rock, and the entire Castle Valley. From our perch, the valley appears to resemble a large city of rock and sand, a city whose skyscrapers look like giant sandcastles. Situated prominently in the middle of the valley is Castle Rock. When Castle Rock is viewed from Porcupine Rim Trail, one notices the standing profile of a priest and two nuns—hence, Castle Rock is also known as Priest and Nuns.

About 300 million years ago, the Uncompahgria uplift (a range in the ancestral Rocky Mountains) caused thousands of cubic miles of earth to be washed down its western flanks. This earth moved over much of the area that now lies before you, compressing the area's salty bottom left behind by receding seas. As thousands of cubic miles of earth continued to cover this salty bed, the salt was forced to flow through pressure-alleviating fault blocks. Attaching themselves to these blocks, these massive bodies of salt and rock

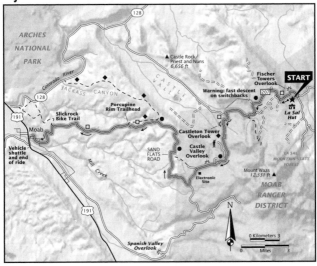

(some of which were 15,000 feet thick) pushed their way upward toward the earth's surface. Nearly 290 million years later, these blocks finally reached the earth's surface in Castle Valley, known in geological circles as a "Salt Valley."

Located within the Colorado Plateau, the vast area of flat-lying sedimentary rock that extends into almost half of Utah and smaller parts of Colorado, Arizona, and New Mexico, Castle Valley offers an exceptional example of these one-time bodies of salt and rock. Under the pressures of tectonic plate shifting ten million years ago, the Colorado Plateau began to rise. Rivers and streams, which had followed a relatively flat course across the plateau, were now pouring through over a vertical mile of sedimentary rock. The layers of sedimentary rock, in turn, receded in the cliffs, as further erosion carved a path for the valley's formation and exposed the massive bodies of salt and rock that had been forming since the Uncompahgre uplift. Once these bodies were exposed to the elements, wind and water dissolved the salt, leaving behind the castles in the valley. Today these formations are made up of mostly calcite, silica, gypsum, and iron oxide, the latter of which gives rise to the castles' ruddy hue. This valley continues to undergo drastic erosion, as these castles made of sand slip back into the "sea," eventually.

Don't let thoughts of cool ocean breezes trick you into thinking it's all downhill to Moab. From your seagull's perch above Castle Valley, descend briefly before climbing two switchback sections, 5 miles in length, to Sand Flats Road and Porcupine Rim Trail. Once you turn onto Sand Flats Road, descend over loose sand and rock for roughly 11 miles, before intersecting with Porcupine Rim Trail. If you're blown out at this point, finish your seven-day tour on Sand Flats Road. For those of you who have a bit more spunk left, bear right onto Porcupine Rim Trail. Either way, enjoy—you got away!

Miles and Directions

0.0 START from the La Sal Hut. Backtrack to Forest Road 207.

0.1 Bear left onto FR 207, heading toward a T intersection.

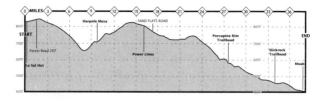

0.2 Arrive at the T intersection, marked by the sign MOAB—38 and NORTH BEAVER MESA—4.5. Bear left (west), following signs for Moab.

0.8 See incredible views of Fischer Towers, to your right.

8.1 Arrive at the head of Castle Valley, with a sign reading MOAB—30 and LA SAL MOUNTAIN LOOP ROAD and OOWAH LAKE, WARNER CAMP-GROUND, MOAB. Bear left, onto the La Sal Mountain Loop Road, and begin climbing.

9.3 Enjoy a fantastic view of Castleton Tower, to your right.

10.1 Reach Harpole Mesa. Here begins a steady switchback climb on pavement.

13.7 Reach the end of the pavement as the road continues to climb moderately.

14.3 Pavement begins again.

16.6 Cross under the power lines. To your left are the communication towers. A fast descent to Moab awaits.

17.0 Passing an OOWAH LAKE sign, to your left, intersect with County Road 67 (Sand Flats Road), to your right. Bear right onto Sand Flats Road, a rough four-wheel-drive road. Look to the distant west and see the Blues (or Abajos), the Henrys (the last mountains to be surveyed in the continental United States), and Navajo Mountain.

20.6 Stay on Sand Flats Road as it parallels a shallow rock canyon to the left, and enter the national forest.

26.0 Pass the unmarked Porcupine Rim Cutoff Trail, to your right.

28.1 Pass the trailhead for Porcupine Rim, to your right, marked by stock troughs with water from a spring, and continue down Sand Flats Road. **Option:** For those wanting to enjoy the great singletrack descent of Porcupine Rim, bear right here. This technically and physically challenging trail will eventually lead to Utah Highway 128 and the Colorado River. From there one may ride in a southwesterly direction to

Taking in the view of Castle Valley.

Moab or arrange to be picked up at the trail's terminus on UT 128. A good place for shuttle vehicles to park would be at the Negro Bill Canyon Trailhead, located off UT 128, less than a quarter mile southwest of Porcupine Rim Trail's terminus. Arranging to be picked up is highly recommended.

34.2   Pavement begins.

34.7   Pass the Slickrock Trailhead, to your right.

37.2   Sand Flats Road turns into Mill Creek Drive.

37.6   Reach the intersection of Mill Creek Drive and 400 East Street, by Dave's Corner Market. Bear right onto 400 East Street.

37.9   Reach the intersection of 400 East Street and 100 South Street. Bear left onto 100 South Street.

38.4   Reach the intersection of 100 South Street and Main Street. Continue for another block and a half west on 100 South Street to the municipal parking lot and your vehicle, ending your weeklong odyssey.

Mountain Biking Basic Essentials

Within the following pages, you will find everything you need to know to have a safe and comfortable off-road bicycling ride. Just because you'll be pedaling way out in the backcountry, don't overlook such important things as bicycling etiquette, rules of the trail, and even rules of the road. And *because* you'll be out in the backcountry, far from convenience stores and quick shelter, this section will detail the items and essentials you'll need to stay safe and comfortable. None of the following lists and advice should replace good old-fashioned common sense, but it may help you understand some of the things you'll want to bring with you before you're too far along and experience something unexpected or unfortunate.

Please note that the following information is especially useful for single-day outings, and does not attempt to cover all of the details of extended off-road overnight trip planning. You should consult with your trip leader or guide service for a detailed list of items, extra clothing, supplies, and support that will be needed or will be provided before you leave.

Mountain Biking Etiquette

Rules of the Trail

If every mountain biker always yielded the right-of-way, stayed on the trail, avoided wet or muddy trails, never cut switchbacks, always rode in control, showed respect for other trail users, and carried out every last scrap of what was carried in (candy wrappers and bike-part debris included)—in short, if we all did the right things—we wouldn't need a list of rules governing our behavior.

The fact is, most mountain bikers are conscientious and are trying to do the right thing; however, thousands of miles of dirt trails have been closed due to the irresponsible habits of a few riders.

Here are some basic guidelines adapted from the International Mountain Bicycling Association Rules of the Trail. These guidelines can help prevent damage to land, water, plants, and wildlife; maintain trail access; and avoid conflicts with other backcountry visitors and trail users.

1. Only ride on trails that are open. Don't trespass on private land, and be sure to obtain any necessary permits. If you're not sure if a trail is closed or if you need a permit, don't hesitate to ask. The way you ride will influence trail management decisions and policies. Federal and state wilderness areas are always off-limits to cycling.

2. Keep your bicycle under control. Watch the condition of the trail at all times, and follow the appropriate speed regulations and recommendations.

3. Yield to others on the trail. Make your approach well known in advance, either with a friendly greeting or a bell. When approaching a corner, junction, or blind spot, expect to encounter other trail users. When passing others, show your respect by slowing to a walking pace.

4. Don't startle animals. Animals may be easily scared by sudden approaches or loud noises. For your safety—and the safety of others in the area as well as the animals themselves—give all wildlife a wide berth. When encountering horses, defer to the horseback riders' directions and dismount on narrow trails.

5. Zero impact. Be aware of the impact you're making on the trail beneath you. You should not ride under conditions where you will leave evidence of your passing, such as on certain soils or shortly after a rainfall. If a ride features optional side hikes into wilderness areas, be a zero-impact hiker too. Whether you're on bike or on foot, stick to existing trails, leave gates as you found them, and carry out everything you brought in.

6. Be prepared. Know the equipment you are using, the area where you'll be riding, and your cycling abilities and limitations. Avoid unnecessary breakdowns by keeping your equipment in good shape. When you head out, bring spare parts and supplies for weather changes. Be sure to wear appropriate safety gear, including a helmet, and learn how to be self-sufficient.

Rules of the Road

Occasionally, even hard-core off-road cyclists will find they have no choice but to ride the pavement. Laws vary by state, but outlined below are a few rules to follow no matter where you ride.

- Follow the same driving rules as motorists. Be sure to obey all road signs and traffic lights.
- Ride with the traffic and not against it.
- Wear a helmet and bright clothing so you are more visible to motorists. Bright colors such as orange and lime green are also highly visible at night.
- Wear a helmet.

- Equip your bike with lights and wear reflective clothing if you plan on riding at night. When riding at night the bicycle or rider should have a white light visible at least 500 feet to the front and a red light or reflector visible at least 600 feet to the rear.

- Ride single file on busy roads so motorists can pass you safely.

- When stopping, be sure to pull completely off the roadway.

- Use hand signals to alert motorists to what you plan on doing next.

- Follow painted lane markings.

- Make eye contact with drivers. Assume they don't see you until you are sure they do.

- Don't ride out to the curb between parked cars unless they are far apart. Motorists may not see you when you try to move back into traffic.

- Turn left by looking back, signaling, getting into the left lane, and turning. In urban situations, continue straight to the crosswalk and walk your bike across the crosswalk when the pedestrian walk sign is illuminated.

- Never ride while under the influence of alcohol or drugs. DUI laws apply when you're riding a bicycle.

- Avoid riding in extremely foggy, rainy, icy, or windy conditions.

- Watch out for parallel-slat sewer grates, slippery manhole covers, oily pavement, gravel, wet leaves, and ice.

- Cross railroad tracks as perpendicular as possible. Be especially careful when it's wet out. For better control as you move across bumps and other hazards, stand up on your pedals.

- Don't ride too close to parked cars—a person opening the car door may hit you.
- Don't ride on sidewalks. Instead, walk your bike. Pedestrians have the right-of-way on all walkways and crosswalks. By law you must give pedestrians audible warning when you pass. Use a bike bell or announce clearly, "On your left/right."
- Slow down at street crossings and driveways.

Clothing

Just as the original mountain bikers headed off in their jeans to hit the trail, mountain bikers can and do wear just about anything to go riding now. There are a few things in the following list that are absolutely necessary and a few that will make your riding more comfortable and more enjoyable.

Be Prepared—Wear Your Armor

It's crucial to discuss the clothing you must wear to be safe, practical, and—if you prefer—stylish. The following is a list of items that will save you from disaster, outfit you comfortably, and most important, keep you looking cool.

Helmet. A helmet is an absolute necessity because it protects your head from complete annihilation. It is the only thing that will not disintegrate into a million pieces after a wicked crash on a descent. A helmet with a solid exterior shell will also protect your head from sharp or protruding objects.

Shorts. These are necessary if you plan to ride your bike more than twenty to thirty minutes. Padded cycling shorts provide cushioning between your body and the bicycle seat, protecting your derriere against serious saddle soreness. There are two types of cycling shorts you can buy. Touring shorts are good for people who don't want to look like they're wearing anatomically correct cellophane. These look like regular athletic shorts with pockets, but they have built-in padding in the crotch area for protection from chafing and saddle sores. The more popular, traditional cycling shorts are made of skintight material, also with a padded crotch. Cycle shorts also wick moisture away from your body and prevent chafing. Whichever style you prefer, cycling shorts are a necessity for long rides.

Gloves. You may find well-padded cycling gloves invaluable when traveling over rocky trails and gravelly roads for hours on end. When you fall off your bike and land on your palms, gloves are your best friend. Long-fingered gloves may also be useful, as branches, trees, assorted hard objects, and, occasionally, small animals will reach out and whack your knuckles. Insulated gloves are essential for winter riding.

Glasses. Not only do sunglasses give you an imposing presence and make you look cool (both are extremely important), they also protect your eyes from harmful ultraviolet rays, invisible branches, creepy bugs, and dirt.

Shoes. Mountain bike shoes are constructed with stiff soles in order to transfer more of the power from a pedal stroke to the drive train and to provide a solid platform on which to stand, thereby decreasing fatigue in your feet. You can use virtually any good, light, outdoor hiking footwear, but specific mountain bike shoes (especially those with inset cleats) are best. They are lighter, breathe better, and are constructed to work with your pedal strokes instead of the natural walking cadence.

Actual armor. If you ride on very technical trails you may want to consider buying some knee-and-shin guards and elbow pads to protect you from whacking your shins on your handlebars and your elbows on the ground.

Dress for the Weather

Layers. It is best to dress in layers that can be added or removed as weather conditions change. When the air has a nip in it, layers will keep the chill away from your chest and help prevent the development of bronchitis. A polypropylene long-sleeved shirt is best to wear against the skin beneath other layers of clothing. Polypropylene, like wool, wicks away moisture from your skin to keep your body dry. The next layer should be a wool or synthetic insulating layer that helps keep you warm but is also breathable. A fleece jacket or vest works well. The outer layer should be a waterproof, windproof, and breathable jacket and pants. Good cold-weather clothing should fit snugly against your body but not be restrictive. Try to avoid wearing cotton or baggy clothing when the temperature falls. Cotton holds moisture like a sponge, and baggy clothing catches cold air and swirls it around your body.

Tights or leg warmers. These are best in temperatures below 55 degrees Fahrenheit. Knees are sensitive and can develop all kinds of problems if they get cold. Common problems include tendinitis, bursitis, and arthritis.

Wool or synthetic socks. These may be helpful in cold weather conditions. Don't pack too many layers under those shoes, though. You may stand the chance of restricting circulation, and your feet will get very cold, very fast.

Thinsulate or Gore-tex gloves. We may all agree that there is nothing worse than frozen feet—unless your hands are frozen. A good pair of Thinsulate or Gore-tex gloves should keep your hands toasty and warm.

Hat or helmet on cold days. Sometimes, when the weather gets really cold and you still want to hit the trails, it's tough to stay warm. We all know that 130 percent of the body's heat escapes through the head, so it's important to keep the cranium warm. Ventilated helmets are designed to keep heads cool in the summer heat, but they do little to help keep heads warm during rides in subzero temperatures. Cyclists should consider wearing a hat on extremely cold days. Fleece skullcaps are great head and ear warmers that fit snugly over your head beneath the helmet. Head protection is not lost. Another option is a helmet cover that covers those ventilating gaps and helps keep the body heat in. These do not, however, keep your ears warm. Your ears will welcome a fleece headband when it's cold out.

All of this clothing can be found at your local bike shop or outdoor retailer, where the staff should be happy to help fit you into gear for the seasons of the year.

Be Prepared—Supplies and Equipment

The Essentials

Remember the Boy Scout motto: Be Prepared. Here are some essential items that will keep you from walking out a long trail, being stranded in the woods, or even losing your life.

First-Aid Kit

- adhesive bandages
- moleskin
- various sterile gauze and dressings
- white surgical tape
- Ace bandage
- antihistamine
- aspirin
- Betadine solution
- a first-aid book
- antacid
- tweezers
- scissors
- antibacterial wipes
- triple-antibiotic ointment
- plastic gloves
- sterile cotton tip applicators
- syrup of ipecac (to induce vomiting)
- thermometer
- wire splint
- matches
- guidebook (In case all else fails and you must start a fire to survive, this guidebook will serve as excellent fire starter!)

Bicycle Repair Kit

- spare tube
- tire irons
- patch kit
- pump
- spoke wrench
- spare spokes to fit your wheel (tape these to the chain stay)
- chain tool
- Allen keys (bring appropriate sizes to fit your bike)
- duct tape

Water. Without it, cyclists may face dehydration, which may result in dizziness and fatigue. On a warm day, cyclists should drink at least one full bottle during every hour of riding. Remember, it's always good to drink before you feel thirsty—otherwise, it may be too late.

Food. This essential item will keep you rolling. Cycling burns up a lot of calories and is among the few sports in which no one is safe from "bonking." Bonking feels like it sounds. Without food in your system, your blood sugar level plummets, and there is no longer any energy in your body. This instantly results in total fatigue, shakiness, and light-headedness. So when you're filling your water bottle, remember to bring along some food. Fruit, energy bars, or some other forms of high-energy food are highly recommended. Candy bars are not, however, because they will deliver a sudden burst of high energy, then let you down soon after, causing you to feel worse than before. Energy bars are available at most grocery stores and bike shops and are similar to candy bars, but they provide complex carbohydrate energy and high nutrition rather than fast-burning simple sugars.

Map and compass. Do not rely solely on the maps in this book. A GPS system is also useful (if you know how to use it), but don't forget the spare batteries. A dead GPS unit is as good as no GPS unit.

To Have or Not to Have—Other Very Useful Items

There is no shortage of items for you and your bike to make riding better, safer, and easier. We have rummaged through the unending lists and separated the gadgets from the good stuff, coming up with what we believe are items certain to make mountain bike riding more enjoyable.

Tires. Buying a good pair of knobby tires is the quickest way to enhance the off-road handling capabilities of a bike. There are many types of mountain bike tires on the market. Some are made exclusively for very rugged off-road terrain. These big-knobbed, soft rubber tires virtually stick to the ground with magnetlike traction, but they tend to deteriorate quickly on pavement. There are other tires made exclusively for the road. These are called "slicks" and have no tread at all. For the average cyclist, though, a good tire somewhere in the middle of these two extremes should do the trick. Realize, however, that you get what you pay for. Do not skimp and buy cheap tires. As your primary point of contact with the trail, tires may be the most important piece of equipment on a bike. With inexpensive rubber, the tire's beads may unravel or chunks of tread actually rip off the tire. If you're lucky, all you'll suffer is a long walk back to the car. If you're unlucky, your tire could blow out in the middle of a rowdy downhill, causing a wicked crash.

Clipless pedals. Clipless pedals, like ski bindings, attach your shoe directly to the pedal. They allow you to exert pressure on the pedals during both the down- and up-strokes. They also help you to maneuver the bike while in the air or climbing various obstacles. Toe clips may be less expensive, but they are also heavier and harder to use. Clipless pedals take a little getting used to, but they're easier to get out of in an emergency than toe clips and are definitely worth the trouble.

Bar ends. These clamp-on additions to your original straight bar will provide more leverage, an excellent grip for climbing, and a more natural position for your hands. Be aware, however, of the bar end's propensity for hooking trees on fast descents, sending you, the cyclist, airborne. Opinions are divided on the general usefulness of bar ends these days, and, over the last few years, bar ends have fallen out of favor with manufacturers and riders alike.

Backpacks and hydration packs. These bags are ideal for carrying keys, extra food and water, guidebooks, foul-weather clothing, tools, spare tubes, a camera, and a cellular phone, in case you need to call for help. If you're carrying lots of equipment, you may want to consider a set of panniers. These are much larger and mount on either side of each wheel on a rack. Keep in mind, however, that with panniers mobility will be severely limited. There are currently a number of streamlined backpacks with hydration systems on the market. Hydration packs are fast becoming an essential item for cyclists pedaling for more than a few hours, especially in hot, dry conditions. Some water packs can carry as much as one hundred ounces of water in their bladder bags. These packs strap on your back with a handy hose running over your shoulder so you can be drinking water while still holding onto the bars with both hands on a rocky descent.

Suspension forks. For off-roaders who want nothing to impede their speed on the trails, investing in a suspension fork can be a good idea. Like tires, there are plenty of brands to choose from, and they all do the same thing—absorb the brutal beatings of a rough trail. The cost of these forks, however, is sometimes more brutal than the trail itself.

Full suspension bikes. Full suspension bikes help smooth out the ride and keep the wheels in contact with the ground. They have been around for a while, but the prices are now falling into a range that the average mountain biker can afford. There are a number of different designs intended for different activities, such as cross-country riding and downhill riding. Be careful when buying and test ride several bikes to determine just what you want.

Bike computers. These are fun gadgets to own and are much less expensive than in years past. They have such features as trip distance, speedometer, odometer, time of day, altitude, alarm, average speed, maximum speed, heart rate, global satellite positioning, etc. Bike computers will come in handy when following these maps or to know just how far you've ridden in the wrong direction.

Last-Minute Checkover

Before a ride, it's a good idea to give your bike a once-over to make sure everything is in working order. Go through the following checklist before each ride to make sure everything is secure and in place.

- **Check the air pressure in your tires to make sure they are properly inflated before each ride.** Mountain bikes require about forty-five to fifty-five pounds per square inch of air pressure. If your tires are underinflated, there is greater likelihood that the tubes may get pinched on a rock, causing the tire to go flat.

- **Pinch the tires to feel for proper inflation.** They should give just a little on the sides but feel very hard on the treads. If you have a pressure gauge, use that.

- **Check your brakes.** Squeeze the rear brake and roll your bike forward. The rear tire should skid. Next, squeeze the front brake and roll your bike forward. The rear wheel should lift into the air. If this doesn't happen, then your brakes are too loose. Make sure the brake levers don't touch the handlebars when squeezed with full force.

- **Check all quick releases on your bike.** Make sure they are all securely tightened. To avoid hooking them on a stick or branch, quick releases should point toward the back of the bike. The front quick release lever should be on the left of the bike and tightened so it runs parallel to the arm of the fork. The back quick release should be closed so it points toward the back of the bike.

- **Lube up.** If your chain squeaks, apply some lubricant.

- **Check your nuts and bolts.** Check the handlebars, saddle, cranks, and pedals to make sure that each is tight and securely fastened to your bike.

- **Check your wheels.** Spin each wheel to see that they spin through the frame and between brake pads freely.

Have you got everything? Make sure you have your spare tube, tire irons, patch kit, frame pump, tools, food, water, foul-weather gear, and guidebook.

Need more info on mountain biking? Consider reading *Basic Essentials Mountain Biking.* You'll discover such things as choosing and maintaining a mountain bike; useful bike-handling techniques; preparing for long rides; overcoming obstacles such as rocks, logs, and water; and even preparing for competition.

Repair and Maintenance

Fixing a Flat

TOOLS YOU WILL NEED

- Two tire irons
- Pump (either a floor pump or a frame pump)
- No screwdrivers!!! (This can puncture the tube.)

REMOVING THE WHEEL

The front wheel is easy. Simply dis-
connect the brake shoes, open the
quick release mechanism or undo the
bolts with the proper sized wrench,
then remove the wheel from the
bike.

   The rear wheel is a little more tricky. Before you loosen
the wheel from the frame, shift the chain into the smallest
gear on the freewheel (the cluster of gears in the back).
Once you've done this, removing and installing the wheel,
like the front, is much easier.

REMOVING THE TIRE

Step one: Insert a tire iron under the bead of the tire and pry
the tire over the lip of the rim. Be careful not to pinch the
tube when you do this.

Step two: Hold the first tire iron in place. With the second
tire iron, repeat step one, 3 or 4 inches down the rim. Alter-

nate tire irons, pulling the bead of the tire over the rim, section by section, until one side of the tire bead is completely off the rim.

Step three: Remove the rest of the tire and tube from the rim. This can be done by hand. It's easiest to remove the valve stem last. Once the tire is off the rim, pull the tube out of the tire.

CLEAN AND SAFETY CHECK

Step four: Using a rag, wipe the inside of the tire to clean out any dirt, sand, glass, thorns, etc. These may cause the tube to puncture. The inside of a tire should feel smooth. Any pricks or bumps could mean that you have found the culprit responsible for your flat tire.

Step five: Wipe the rim clean, then check the rim strip, making sure it covers the spoke nipples properly on the inside of the rim. If a spoke is poking through the rim strip, it could cause a puncture.

Step six: At this point, you can do one of two things: replace the punctured tube with a new one, or patch the hole. It's easiest to just replace the tube with a new tube when you're out on the trails. Roll up the old tube and take it home to repair later that night in front of the TV. Directions on patching a tube are usually included with the patch kit itself.

INSTALLING THE TIRE AND TUBE

(This can be done entirely by hand.)

Step seven: Inflate the new or repaired tube with enough air to give it shape, then tuck it back into the tire.

Step eight: To put the tire and tube back on the rim, begin by putting the valve in the valve hole. The valve must be straight. Then use your hands to push the beaded edge of the tire onto the rim all the way around so that one side of your tire is on the rim.

Step nine: Let most of the air out of the tube to allow room for the rest of the tire.

Step ten: Beginning opposite the valve, use your thumbs to push the other side of the tire onto the rim. Be careful not to pinch the tube in between the tire and the rim. The last few inches may be difficult, and you may need the tire iron to pry the tire onto the rim. If so, just be careful not to puncture the tube.

BEFORE INFLATING COMPLETELY

Step eleven: Check to make sure the tire is seated properly and that the tube is not caught between the tire and the rim. Do this by adding about five to ten pounds of air, and watch closely that the tube does not bulge out of the tire.

Step twelve: Once you're sure the tire and tube are properly seated, put the wheel back on the bike, then fill the tire with air. It's easier squeezing the wheel through the brake shoes if the tire is still flat.

Step thirteen: Now fill the tire with the proper amount of air, and check constantly to make sure the tube doesn't bulge from the rim. If the tube does appear to bulge out, release all the air as quickly as possible, or you could be in for a big bang. Place the wheel back in the dropout and tighten the quick release lever. Reconnect the brake shoes.

When installing the rear wheel, place the chain back onto the smallest cog (farthest gear on the right), and pull the derailleur out of the way. Your wheel should slide right on.

Lubrication Prevents Deterioration

Lubrication is crucial to maintaining your bike. Dry spots will be eliminated. Creaks, squeaks, grinding, and binding will be gone. The chain will run quietly, and the gears will shift smoothly. The brakes will grip quicker, and your bike may last longer with fewer repairs. Need I say more? Well, yes. Without knowing where to put the lubrication, what good is it?

THINGS YOU WILL NEED

- One can of bicycle lubricant, found at any bike store
- A clean rag (to wipe excess lubricant away)

WHAT GETS LUBRICATED

- Front derailleur
- Rear derailleur
- Shift levers
- Front brake
- Rear brake
- Both brake levers
- Chain

WHERE TO LUBRICATE

To make it easy, simply spray a little lubricant on all the pivot points of your bike. If you're using a squeeze bottle, use just a drop or two. Put a few drops on each point wherever metal moves against metal, for instance, at the center of the brake calipers. Then let the lube sink in.

Once you have applied the lubricant to the derailleurs, shift the gears a few times, working the derailleurs back and forth. This allows the lubricant to work itself into the tiny cracks and spaces it must occupy to do its job. Work the brakes a few times as well.

LUBING THE CHAIN

Lubricating the chain should be done after the chain has been wiped clean of most road grime. Do this by spinning the pedals counterclockwise while gripping the chain with a clean rag. As you add the lubricant, be sure to get some in between each

link. With an aerosol spray, just spray the chain while pedaling backwards (counterclockwise) until the chain is fully lubricated. Let the lubricant soak in for a few seconds before wiping the excess away. Chains will collect dirt much faster if they're loaded with too much lubrication.

About the Author

Stephen Hlawaty lives with his family in Livermore, Colorado, where he enjoys year-round outdoor bliss: from skiing Cameron Pass in the winter, to mountain biking and camping in Roosevelt National Forest in the spring and summer, to chopping wood alongside his home in the fall. When not offering his blood, sweat, and tears in these outdoor pursuits, he can often be found on his back porch pickin' and slidin' on his Regal Reso.